Pens on Fire

*Creative Writing Experiments
for Teens from WriteGirl*

www.writegirl.org

WriteGirl Publications

Los Angeles

INTRODUCTION

Keren Taylor, *Editor*:

Teaching creative writing to teens can be challenging. WriteGirl has techniques to get even the most reluctant pens moving. Creative writing is not just for those who are creative – it is a doorway to empowerment, confidence, and academic success for all students. Most schools and programs focus on academic writing, including grammar, spelling, and exposition. Often, only the most accomplished academic writers have an opportunity to participate in creative writing, and few of those students are provided with adequate writing tools, skills, and guidance and then given the freedom to create on their own. The WriteGirl program is different. It is designed to empower the creative writer in all students, which will, in turn, improve their confidence in academic writing and in themselves.

Imparting sufficient writing skills for all students continues to be a national challenge, whether students are struggling to succeed in overcrowded urban districts or striving for excellence in suburban areas that have long records of achievement. Young people are spending increasing amounts of time interfacing with television, video games, computers, cellphones, and ipods, and a decreasing amount of time reading and writing. According to the November 2007 National Endowment for the Arts study, *To Read or Not To Read: A Question of National Consequence*, a comprehensive analysis of reading patterns in the United States, less than 1/3 of thirteen-year-olds are daily readers, a 14% decline from 20 years earlier. Among seventeen-year-olds, the percentage of non-readers doubled over a 20 year period from 9% in 1984 to 19% in 2004.

More robust and innovative curriculum in language arts is critical for turning around these frightening statistics. Engaging young people in reading and writing is extremely difficult, given the fast-paced, 24-images-per-second, 30-text-messages-per-hour, multi-media world they inhabit.

We have found that students do love to write, given the right environment and stimulation. What we have learned at WriteGirl is that writing becomes fun when it is game-like and playful. We use the word "experiment" instead of "exercise." We ask writers to "share their words" instead of "perform their work." We approach revision with energy, passing out neon pens, sticky notes, and even scissors. We use colorful posters, index cards, photographs, newspapers, props, videos, and music to inspire curiosity and imagination.

We see that teens become most engaged when we ask them to write about areas where they are experts, such as themselves, their neighborhoods, their families, and their unique experiences and opinions. Over and over again, the themes of identity, community, and culture prove to be deep wells for finding stories and making personal discoveries.

This book is easy to use; it is designed specifically for teachers and workshop leaders who have limited time to plan lessons outside of their required curricula. Goals, materials, and setup needs for each activity are clearly and simply presented, and each experiment is broken into distinct steps. It's plug-and-play, or should we say, "write-and-play."

The activities in this book are tested and have been proven highly effective. Each experiment is followed by examples of student writing with annotations offering specific insights into the writing process and our approach. We have included space on each experiment page for teachers to make notes for adapting these activities to their specific classrooms.

While our focus is working with teens, many of these writing experiments are suitable for middle school students and even adults. Experiments can be modified to work one-on-one with an individual writer, or with a group as large as 100!

The final chapter of the book, "Zippers," offers a wide selection of quick writing activities for students which require no preparation at all. They can be handed out in class, given as take-home activities, posted on the wall, or even taped under a table or chairs for a surprise.

We hope that this book of creative writing experiments will give you not only specific lesson plans, but also tools and techniques for inspiring both boys and girls to put their ideas, perspectives, and stories into words.

Kim Purcell, *Editor*:

The main reason we wrote this curriculum guide is to help make writing fun for teens. If people are bored, they don't absorb information; they zone out. In all the years that I've been teaching, I've found this to be true for adults as well as litttle toddlers. At WriteGirl, we try to make the writing workshops enjoyable and stimulating to all types of learners. At WriteGirl, we don't give long lessons on structure or the mechanics of writing. We let the writers learn by doing, and we encourage them to read.

In every section of this guide, we have interviews from experts in each field. These experts share their experiences and advice, as well as a reading list. We hope your writers will be inspired by these interviews.

Throughout this guide, you will see that we call the participants "writers" because we believe that everyone is a writer, just at different stages of development. Everyone has the potential to write beautifully, and everyone can become an archaeologist of (his or) her own experience once they learn to dig inside. We've found that once people start accessing their personal stories and learn how to make their writing come alive with vibrant details, every piece they write will improve, from essays to poetry.

Table of Contents

CREATIVE NONFICTION EXPERIMENTS

A few words from creative nonfiction expert Sara Kaye Larson:

Sara Kaye Larson is a web designer, video creator, and writer. She manages several websites, including multi-media projects, a new travel site, and *The Office Sign Project* (a web-based photo collaboration). She is a zinester (of {inset name}) and an advocate for alternative media. While in grad school, she worked exclusively in film and video. Her documentary premiered in the Kodak Emerging Filmmaker Program at Cannes International Film Festival in 2005.

What exactly is creative nonfiction? What makes it different from other genres?

Using the term "creative nonfiction" makes it sound like regular ol' nonfiction isn't creative. Nearly all writing (except, in my opinion, filling out applications) is creative – you are creating something from nothing. Creative nonfiction is also called literary journalism or narrative journalism. It is the writing of factual events, experiences, and measurements using elements of fiction writing. Creative nonfiction focuses on setting, developed characters, sights, sounds, smells, and suspense. You tell a true story that reads like *The Da Vinci Code*.

What are the special components of creative nonfiction?

Unlike an AP-style newspaper article, a creative nonfiction piece has a distinct viewpoint and voice. Creative nonfiction writers often reveal the author either through direct or stylistic reference. You know what I am talking about if you have ever read an interview in *Rolling Stone* and the writer keeps interjecting how he got to sit next to Christina Aguilera, or when the author is submerged in the story and lets you know it. Think about Hunter S. Thompson and Truman Capote, for example.

How did you get into creative nonfiction?

Ever since I passed my first note in class, I have been writing creative nonfiction. And ever since I saved every note I ever got, I have been interested in documentation.

What sort of writing habits/schedule do you keep?

I write in some form or another just about every day. I have a "Dear Diary" type journal where I write pure babbling stuff that I would be embarrassed if anyone found. I have tons of those dollar-store spiral-bound 3x5 notebooks on hand in my purse in case I see someone or something interesting. And once that is out of the way, I get to working on one of the projects that I have going on, my websites, or a script. It's shocking to hear, but writing is truly about 99% discipline. I think it was the great Curtis Mayfield who said his work consisted of 2% jazz and 98% funky stuff. Or was it 2% perspiration, 98% inspiration… you could go on and on.

Where do you look for inspiration?

I look for inspiration in everything. Some writers like to write about hope, , and beauty. I find these things very inspiring for living, but when it comes to writing, I prefer a darker side. I have used creative nonfiction in order to cope with difficult people and difficult situations. I write about jobs that I don't like, medical treatments I have had to suffer through, embarrassing situations, people who don't appreciate my Christmas presents, and anything else I would rather not deal with. If you cross me, you are running the risk of a very sarcastic and cutting essay being written about you disguised as a magazine article entitled "How to Turn a Friend Down for Dinner Without Hurting Her Feelings." But really, all things in your life can inspire you. You are probably an expert on at least a few things; like, for example, only you know how much milk you like in your cereal. Write about it. Just include great details and honest information.

How would you recommend we get started writing a creative nonfiction piece?

Lists are always a great way to start. List five ways to, say, skin a cat or pick out the best lip gloss. After you write a quick list, add on to each item extra information and detail.

Take a newsworthy story in your life (like you just won an arm wrestling contest) and concentrate on one aspect of it. Really concentrate on the sound and tone of it, or the smell of it. Set up the people in the story as if they were a cast of characters.

Start up a blog. You can create your own blog on blogspot.com. If you have a camera, take some pictures of stuff you see throughout your day and write about it. Be sure to give the reader some insight into how you see and experience your day. Make it so that only you could have written it.

Reading is a big part of writing. Recommended reading?

Zelda, Band of Brothers, any Thomas Wolfe or Hunter S. Thompson, Amy Sedaris, Chuck Klosterman, Ian Frazier…

In addition to zines (http://www.factsheet5.org/), I read *Harper's* and *Bitch* magazines and whatever else is in the waiting room.

When it comes to creative fiction…

Always:
Keep your eyes and ears open.
Write about what you like or what you have a strong opinion on.
Publish yourself whenever you have the chance.
Have snacks handy.

Never:
Think that taking a specific point of view makes something not true.

School Lunch Stories

Experiment:
Writers explore school lunch as a jumping-off point for writing a personal story.

Goal:
Create a captivating piece of creative nonfiction through attention to specific details.

Materials:
Two posters, markers, tape to put the posters up (or easels),
a piece of paper that will cover the surface of one poster.

Setup:
On poster #1, write:

- What were the various foods you ate during last school lunch? List each item.

- How would you describe the characteristics of each of those items?
  (shiny, sticky, clumpy, sweet, dry, etc.)

On poster #2, list provocative questions to help writers find the story around their lunch.

Suggested questions:
- Who did you sit/eat with?

- Why did you sit with that person or those people?

- What did you talk about?

- Who made your lunch?

- Describe how you enjoyed or hated your lunch.

*Poster #2 should be covered up until the dramatic reveal at the start
of Experiment Step 2, below.*

Experiment Steps:

1. Ask the group to write answers to the questions on poster #1. Instruct them to
   report just the basic information in a factual way, without adding any opinions.

2. Unveil poster #2. Using the prompts from poster #2, ask writers to write down
   the true story of what happened during that lunch. Use many of the factual details
   from the first set of questions on poster #1 n the story.

3. Ask writers to share their stories out loud. Choose to read as many of the School
   Lunch pieces as time allows.

Ideas and Notes:

Not Just the Facts, Ma'am

Experiment:

Pairs read, write, and transform back-cover biographies for one another.

Goal:

Revise and enhance a simple piece of writing through interviews.

Materials:

A selection of nonfiction books with photos and bios of the authors in the back of the books. (One book needed per pair of writers.)

Setup:

Display the nonfiction books on a browsing table.

Experiment Steps:

1. Pair writers up.

2. Give each pair a few moments to look over the books on the browsing table and select a book. (One per pair.)

3. Have the pair read the author's bio together.

4. Ask each writer to write their own two-to-three sentence biography, in a similar style to the bio they just read.

5. Have the writers interview each other for a few minutes, writing down their partner's answers.

6. After the interviews, writers exchange their biographies. Each writer expands or rewrites their partner's biography using information they learned during their interviews with each other.

7. Each will take a turn reading their new and improved partner's bio to their partner. Or, they can read the bios to the entire group, time permitting.

Ideas and Notes:

Personal Artifacts

Experiment:
Explore the things we save and why we save them.

Goal:
Develop a brief essay about a personal object.

Materials:
A collection of unique objects (for example: a seashell, a wooden statue, a carved box, a foreign coin, etc.). Include items that are natural, man-made, old, and new.

Setup:
Display the collection of objects on a table, ideally on a brightly-colored tablecloth.

Experiment Steps:

1. Give writers a few minutes to browse the items on the display table.

2. Ask writers to think of things that they save. It can be a single thing or a whole collection of stuff (like a stuffed animal from childhood or a sticker collection). Encourage writers to list as many items or collections that they can think of.

3. Have writers circle one item/collection on their list.

4. Have writers write down their answers to a series of questions about that particular object or collection. Allow writers to write for about 30 seconds after each question.

   Suggested brainstorming questions:
   - How did you save it? (In a shoebox? Under Plexiglas?)
   - Why do you think you saved it?
   - What would other people think if they found your item or collection?
   - How long will you keep it? Is it for sale?
   - Do you try to seek out other people who save the same stuff?
   - Does the item express your personality?
   - Does it prove you went somewhere or that something existed?

5. Give writers some time to write a few paragraphs using any or all of their answers.

6. Have writers share their stories in small groups of 5 to 6 or as a whole group. Offer brief and positive feedback to each writer.

Ideas and Notes:

Cultural Connections

Experiment:

Explore our affinity groups and discover the expert knowledge we have of specific customs, rituals, language, etc. through involvement in these groups.

Goal:

Show writers how they are already experts and how they can use their unique firsthand experiences to create personal essays.

Setup:

Introduce the idea of cultures or affinity groups and ask writers to think about the kinds of groups they belong to, such as their cultural heritage, clubs, sports, hobbies, games, activities, causes or music choices. If you lead a group discussion, it can be helpful to write their responses on a poster.

Experiment Steps:

1. Ask writers to list the various cultures and groups that they belong to or with whom they identify.

2. Have writers select one of those groups or cultures and list all the words or phrases that are specific to that group, including slang or foreign words and phrases. Ask them to list the specific words and phrases they might use to communicate with other people in that group.

3. Once writers have generated at least ten words and/or phrases, ask them to write a short paragraph using as many of the words on the list as they can to describe and introduce someone to this culture or group.

4. Have writers share their writing with the group, and ask the group to try to guess the expert words and phrases the writer used.

Ideas and Notes:

Scents of Home

Experiment:

Use scents to stir up a scene or an entire story.

Goal:

Write an attention grabbing scene or story inspired by a specific scent.

Setup:

Fill 10 bottles/containers with different spices, oils, or lotions.
You can also use fragrant candles.

Experiment Steps:

1. Ask writers to pass around the scent bottles or candles and smell the items IN SILENCE. It might be helpful to turn down the lights to encourage a quiet atmosphere.

2. Ask them to select and focus on one scent.

3. Ask questions for them to answer about the scent they chose.

   Some suggested questions:
   - Where in your home might you find this scent?
   - How does it make you feel?
   - What does it remind you of? What memories of home come up?
   - List as many adjectives as you can that describe this scent.
   - Invent a name for this scent.

   Allow some time for the writers to answer each question.

4. Ask writers to write a paragraph using many of the words they have written.

Ideas and Notes:

Travel Writing

Experiment:

Have you ever been to another country? Traveled to a different city?
Walked to a different neighborhood? Ever left your house? If you can answer
"yes" to any of these questions, you can write a travel piece.

Goal:

Using simple steps, write about a place you have traveled to.

Materials:

Some objects the leader collected while traveling.
Another option: Writers bring something they collected while traveling.

Experiment Steps:

1. Show something you brought from a trip and talk about what it means to you and how
   it could be used in a travel piece. Writers may also talk about objects they brought.

2. As they brainstorm about the journey, read out the following questions: How did you get
   to where you were going? Did you take a plane? Ride a donkey? Walk there? Tell us if
   your feet were aching, or if your legs were cramped on the train there.

3. Ask writers to begin a paragraph about their physical experience during their journey.

4. Read out the following questions to help writers brainstorm about the arrival. Ask writers
   to jot down notes about memories that come to them. What happened when you got there?
   What did you see? What did you experience?

5. Using all five senses, have writers draft a paragraph about the destination.

6. Read the following questions about the surprises/memories/your insights to get writers
   to brainstorm: Did anything unexpected happen on your trip? Did you learn something?
   What will you take away with you (beyond physical souvenirs)? What do you remember
   most about your trip?

7. Writers finish the piece by writing about their psychological/emotional/internal experience.

8. Ask writers to share their writing with the group.

Ideas and Notes:

What You Keep

Experiment:

What people collect at the end of a week in their backpack or purse says a lot about them. Old receipts, menus, bus stubs, phone numbers, directions are all part of the documentation of where they've been or plan to go. In this experiment, writers examine the "documents" they keep to reveal their identities, hopes, dreams, and fears.

Goal:

Look at the fast pace of our lives. Tap into our memories to examine the conscious or unconscious paths we take in life.

Materials:

Leader brings an assortment of menus, receipts, junk mail. Writers add to this assortment by taking something out of their own bags, pockets, and purses.

Experiment Steps:

1. Have each writer select a document that appeals to them.

2. Ask writers to start by describing its literal use. For example, "This menu is for a Chinese restaurant in L.A.'s Chinatown." Then, have writers do some associative or automatic writing about a particular experience they had related to that kind of document; for example, a particular item they bought, memorable meal they had or event they went to. ("Mongolian food is full of strange smells and tastes, and I never felt particularly adventurous until that Saturday when…")

3. Remind writers to be as specific as possible about that experience and use sensory details: smell, taste, touch, sound, sight. Tell them that the document, while not something they collected themselves, opens a door to a moment in time absolutely worth writing down in as much exquisite detail as they can muster.

4. Writers read their pieces aloud, showing the object that inspired the piece.

Ideas and Notes:

Food and Family

Experiment:
Write about family through exploring food and family gatherings.

Goal:
Use the plethora of food stories from your family to write a creative nonfiction piece.

Materials:
Homemade food to hand out to the group, an apron.

Experiment Steps:

1. Hand out food to the class and talk about the recipe and how it developed in your family. It can be simple or elaborate. For example, you might bring cut-up pieces of bread, butter and chocolate sprinkles, and talk about how this was a standard breakfast in your Dutch family.

2. Read a food piece to the group. (Recommended: *Eating Korean* by Cecilia Lee)

3. Ask writers to brainstorm about the dishes they ate at home, anything that was not pre-made or take-out.

4. Have writers draft a story about this food, the preparation, the people who prepared or ate it, and the activities and events around this food. Encourage writers to describe all the sensory details about the food: appearance, sound, texture, taste, and smell.

5. Have writers share their stories with the whole group.

Ideas and Notes:

JOURNALISM
EXPERIMENTS

A few words from journalism expert Erika Hayasaki:

Erika Hayasaki is staff reporter for the *Los Angeles Times* where she specializes in writing about education and youth. She won the 2004 *Los Angeles Times* Best Writing Award for her stories about a new teacher's plight, a boy's dangerous journey to school, and a cultural divide at a Latino high school. In that same year, she was a finalist for the National Livingston Awards for Young Journalists. In 2006, Hayasaki was a recipient of the American Society of Newspaper Editors' Team Breaking News Award for coverage of the Metrolink train crash in Glendale, California.

What is journalism? What makes it different from other genres?

Journalism is reporting stories about the world around us. It involves gathering facts and interviewing people. Every story must be based on facts, research, and observations. Journalists seek truth. They ask questions about why things happen. They hold leaders accountable for their decisions. They point out issues or problems in society. They part the curtain on areas of the world that people may not understand.

How did you get into journalism?

I became a journalist at 15. It was after my parents divorced and I moved across the country with my mother and brother. I did not have friends in my new school. I cut classes and I ate lunch alone in a bathroom stall. I earned Ds and Fs. I was angry and depressed.

One day, the dean suspended me for smoking a cigarette on campus. I remember sitting in my room the next day, grounded. I had an assignment for my newspaper class to write something. Anything. I had to do it or I would flunk. I figured I had nothing better to do, so I began to write. Out of my heart came an article. It was a personal story of when I was ridiculed and hated as a mixed-race child who had grown up in a segregated, small Midwestern town.

Over the next few years, I learned how to tell stories about life. I became the editor of the school newspaper and I wrote a column for a *Seattle Times'* teen newspaper. My articles made people cry and they made people angry.

I earned college scholarships for journalism, even though I had ruined my first two years of high school with bad grades. I went on to the University of Illinois, where I majored in the field. In college, I wrote for the campus newspaper. I also got my first real job writing obituaries for the local city newspaper. During the summer, I interned at newspapers in Seattle, and Florida. At age 21, I landed my dream job at the *Los Angeles Times*.

I will never stop telling stories about life. I believe good journalism makes us think and feel. It connects us to this world and to each other.

How do you pick what to write about? Where do you look for inspiration?

When you work at a newspaper, you usually have an assignment called a "beat." A beat means you are responsible for covering a subject matter such as health, city government, science, music, religion. Your beat could also be covering an entire region like Orange County or New York or Iraq. When I got hired at the *Los Angeles Times*, editors assigned me the education beat. I was responsible for writing stories about Los Angeles schools. That meant covering school board meetings, writing about the superintendent, finding stories about principals and teachers. I did all of that, or; but I soon discovered that I felt most passionate about the stories I wrote involving children inside the schools.

Now I mostly write stories about children and teenagers. I am fascinated by young people whose lives represent something bigger than they can even imagine. For example, in 2005, editors requested a group of reporters work on a project examining why so many students in Los Angeles Unified School District drop out of school. I hung out at a Denny's restaurant where I met a group of teenage boys. The twelve of them grew up together and were best friends. By their senior year, nine had dropped out of school. Their painful stories put a face on the dropout issue.

I start with an issue I want to explore, then I go to places where I will find people who can help me understand it. I wander around talking to people until I find the perfect subjects, or "characters," as they say in fiction writing.

What is the life cycle/timeline of an article?

Some articles take a few hours to report and write; others take a few months or even years. If your editors give you a daily assignment, that means you have to turn the story around in a day. You will have to interview people immediately and write the story on a deadline. Some stories require a few months of interviewing people, combing through documents, and shadowing people you are writing about.

How would you recommend that someone get started in journalism?

Join your high school newspaper. Think of your community as the setting for a million stories. Hang out in new places. Think about what you care about. What makes you angry? What do you want people to pay attention to? What fascinates you? Talk to everyone. What are the stories you want to tell? Read the newspaper every day. Write emails to reporters whose work you admire. Maybe they will take you for coffee one day. Keep files of articles that inspire you.

Look for journalism programs, scholarships, and internships. Write articles for *L.A. Youth*, a local teen newspaper. Ask a small community newspaper if you can freelance some articles or maybe even write some articles for free. Get a lot of clips. Get a lot of experience. This is a job that you learn by doing. You also have to read a lot. Reading will help you become a better writer.

When it comes to journalism…

Always:

Be curious and ask lots of questions.

Triple-check everything.

Challenge yourself to dig deeper.

Read a lot.

Present a balanced story (interview all sides).

Never:

Lie or misrepresent yourself. Don't go "under cover."

Don't tell people you're not a reporter in order to get a story. It is unethical.

Never make things up or plagiarize.

Do not accept gifts or bribes from people you are writing about.

Is This News to You?

Experiment:

Conduct a survey to determine how and where teens get their news.

Goal:

Identify the various sources for news and examine news-watching patterns.

Materials:

Seven posters, markers.

Setup:

Prepare seven posters with the following headings:

- Where do you get your news? (Five columns: Radio, Internet, TV, Magazines, Newspapers.) Instruct writers to put their initials in as many columns as appropriate.

- How often do you read or watch the news? (Four columns: Daily, A Few Times a Week, Once a Week, Once a Month.) Instruct writers to initial in only one column.

- What news story are you following now?

- Do you read or listen to the news in another language? If so, what language?

- Do you trust the news? (Two columns: Yes, No.) Instruct writers to initial in one of the columns.

- Who are your favorite journalists?

- What issues would you like to read about in the news?

Experiment Steps:

1. Give writers some time to write on each of the posters.

2. Ask writers to spend a few minutes with each poster and write down their observations about the responses.

3. Discuss the findings as a group.

Ideas and Notes:

It's All in the Details

Experiment:

Write a vivid article from personal observation.

Goal:

Explore how specific sensory details can bring a story to life.

Materials:

One poster.

Setup:

Prepare a poster listing some of the elements of effective reporting.

Suggested elements:

- Show, rather than tell, what is going on.

- Use strong visual imagery.

- Describe sensory details so readers feel, see, hear, taste, and smell the world of the story.

- Little details are often the most powerful parts of a story.

Experiment Steps:

1. Discuss the elements of effective reporting on the poster. Instruct them to use all of their senses to describe what they notice and have them write down all the details.

2. Take writers outside for five minutes of silent observation and writing.

3. Return inside and have writers create a news article based on the notes they wrote. Ask them to write a headline for their article.

4. Have writers share their pieces with the group. Ask the group to identify the various sensory details in the writing.

Ideas and Notes:

Know Your Audience

Experiment:
Write a personal profile for a magazine.

Goal:
Investigate how the audience for a specific magazine can change the tone and angle of a story.

Materials:
Copies of various kinds of magazines, such as *Seventeen*, *TIME*, and *Sports Illustrated*.

Experiment Steps:

1. Ask writers to think of three provocative and personal questions they wish someone would ask them. (Some suggested questions: "What makes you get up in the morning?" "Who do you love most in the world?" "What frustrates you the most about your school?")

2. Have writers answer the questions as if they were being interviewed.

3. Ask writers to write a short magazine article based on that interview.

4. Have the writers rewrite the article for two completely different magazines, keeping in mind the kind of people who read those magazines. Encourage them to change the questions, add details as needed, adjust the tone and rhythm of the wording, and expand sections while keeping the information factual.

5. Have readers share their writing, and ask the group to guess what magazines they imagined they were writing for.

Ideas and Notes:

Eyes Up

Experiment:

Interview a subject using active listening, personal shorthand, and trigger words.

Goal:

Improve interviewing skills.

Setup:

Leader should prepare a written speech describing at least twenty details about a specific place that the leader is very familiar with, such as a park, beach, restaurant, or grocery store.

Experiment Steps:

1. Have writers stand up with their notebooks in their hands. Instruct them to take notes as you speak to them, without looking down at their page. Encourage them to try to come up with their own form of shorthand, writing down abbreviations and trigger words that will help them remember what they heard.

2. Read your speech to the group quickly.

3. Ask the writers to try to recreate all the details of your speech.

4. Have writers share their versions with the group.

Variation:

Allow writers to ask the leader questions to gather even more details.

Ideas and Notes:

SCREENWRITING
EXPERIMENTS

A few words from screenwriting expert Jennifer Hoppe:

When she was a sophomore in high school, Jennifer Hoppe wrote a one-act play that her mother threw away along with some school papers and field day ribbons, but maybe that wasn't such a bad thing. When she was in her twenties, she moved from Texas to Los Angeles and began trying to break into TV or film, whichever came first. It was film, and that wasn't until she was in her 30s. She's made a living as a writer for 10 years and has written scripts for almost every major studio. She works with a writing partner and they are now on the brink of a career in television, so new adventures await.

What exactly is screenwriting? What makes it different from other genres?

Screenwriting is the art of writing movies. The challenge is in telling your story in pictures, usually in under 120 pages, always within a three-act structure: the first act is 30 pages, the second 60, and the third 30. Aside from this fairly rigid structure, what makes screenwriting different from other forms is that screenplays must be visual. The rule is that no one goes to see a movie to watch characters talk or think. Exceptions exist, but by and large, characters in screenplays have to "do." For instance, if we show a guy get up in the morning and trudge through his filthy apartment to make coffee, but the can is empty so he fishes a used filter out of the trash and makes his coffee with that, you get in less than a minute who this guy is, right? It's a picture. Better yet, if he is a cop and the movie is about a murder case, we could show him making coffee this way in the victim's apartment as he talks to his partner about clues. That way, no time is wasted. The thing that makes screenwriting different from other forms of writing is that it's not just about words. It's about the pictures you paint with them.

What are the special components of screenwriting?

Beginning, middle, and end.

Give a character an objective, have her try to achieve that objective, but throw obstacles and opportunities in her way.

Or, as they say, chase a guy up a tree, shake a stick at him, then get him down.

What sort of writing habits/schedule do you keep?

I try to write every day. But I also procrastinate every day, so it takes a while to sit down. I think that's the hardest part of writing – just sitting down.

Where do you look for inspiration?

I look for inspiration everywhere. Yesterday, I was standing behind a guy at Starbucks. His shirt was on inside out and I was obsessed with it. I wanted to tell him, but he was on the phone. Did he do it deliberately? Should I interrupt his call? It was driving me crazy! And I thought, this is a scene. This is how a couple meets. Or how a robbery gets botched. This is a funny way for two strangers to interact. I'm always thinking like that.

How would you recommend we get started writing a screenplay?

Know the story you want to tell. Screenwriting is formulaic, so I suggest reading the book *Screenplay* by Syd Field (that's how I started) so that you know the rudiments of the craft. Many great writers break the rules, but they know those rules before they break them, so understand a screenplay's structure. Understand where the act breaks occur and what needs to happen by what page.

Many things happen to scripts after they're written, but mostly what happens is nothing. Because movies are expensive to make, only a fraction of scripts written actually turn into films, and even those take years. So, if you want to write screenplays, write them because you love to write screenplays.

What do you wish you would have known when you first started screenwriting?

I wish I'd known that finishing one screenplay is just the beginning. I wish I'd known that it's not the writing, it's the rewriting. But one can't know any of that without experiencing it.

Reading is a big part of writing. Can you suggest a few screenplays for us to read?

Read the scripts of movies you've loved. Read as many good scripts as you can. Read bad scripts, too, so you know what not to do. Many screenplays are available for free online. Here are a couple of resources:

http://www.simplyscripts.com

http://sfy.ru

Let the Music Move Ya

Experiment:

Use music to unlock the emotions of a character.

Goal:

To find your character's inner voice.

Materials:

CDs of a wide variety of music and a stereo or ipod.
Photographs of people from magazines.

Experiment Steps:

1. Have writers select a photograph of a person from a magazine.

2. Ask writers to imagine they are the character in the photograph.

3. Play part of a song and ask the writers to imagine what the character is thinking as the character listens to the song. Give writers two minutes to write down the character's thoughts.

4. Repeat step 3, using a different song.

5. Ask writers to share their writing as well as the photograph they chose.

Ideas and Notes:

Who Are You?

Experiment:
Use questions to shape a character.

Goal:
Create a character who is "alive."

Materials:
Posters, markers.

Setup:
Prepare approximately 10 posters with a question on each one.
Select from the following questions or create your own:

- Who do you love?
- When do you feel the most alone?
- What makes you laugh?
- What's your favorite meal?
- What did you dream about last night?
- What song do you sing in the shower?
- Who would you vote for?
- Where were you last night and who were you with? Who can verify that?
- What haven't you done yet that you would like to do?
- What do you like to do on a sunny Sunday morning?
- What bugs you the most about the city/town/place in which you live?
- What is something to which you would never say no?
- Where is your favorite place?
- What has been the most important event in your life?
- What's your nickname?
- What's the stupidest thing you've ever done?
- What makes you wake up screaming?

Experiment Steps:

1. Ask writers to write down the name of a character they would like to develop.

2. Give them 15 minutes to quietly walk around the room with a pad of paper and answer any or all of the questions in their character's voice.

3. Ask writers to share some of their writing with the group.

Ideas and Notes:

What a Scene!

Experiment:
Create scenes using specific settings and conflicts.

Goal:
Write a complete scene that reveals a conflict and a resolution.

Materials:
Two packs of two different-colored index cards. (For a group of 25 writers, you will need 25 index cards in each of the two colors.) Two boxes or baskets.

Experiment Steps:

1. Lead a brainstorming session on the variety of settings/locations where a scene can take place (e.g., the beach, in the kitchen, on the freeway). Give each of the writers an index card of the same color and ask them to write down one setting/location on the card, being as specific as possible.

2. Collect the setting cards and place them in a box or basket.

3. Lead a brainstorming session on the variety of conflicts that can happen in a scene (e.g., breaking up, a robbery, confessing a lie). Give each of the writers an index card of the same color (different from the setting cards), and ask them to write down a conflict on the card.

4. Collect the conflict cards and place them in a box or basket.

5. Ask each writer to draw a setting card and a conflict card from each basket.

6. Using two characters from a story the writer is working on, or from a book the writer is currently reading, or from his or her imagination, ask the writer to construct a dialogue-based scene using the setting and conflict they selected. (Writers may need 15 minutes or longer for this step.)

Extra Option:
   Cast the scenes and have the writers perform them for the whole group.
   Ask the group to guess about the setting and the conflict.

Ideas and Notes:

My Movie Trailer

Experiment:
Create a movie trailer for an imaginary story.

Goal:
Help writers develop storytelling skills by giving them specific parameters and tools for visually depicting the main points of their story.

Materials:
Index cards, card stock, and pencils.

Setup:
Prepare index cards by writing a movie genre on each one (e.g., romantic, horror, Western, comedy, etc.) and place them all in a box.

Experiment Steps:

1. Divide the writers into groups of five to six people each.

2. Ask one member from each group to select a movie genre from the box.

3. Give each group five pieces of card stock (or paper) and discuss the idea of a "storyboard." (A storyboard is a series of panels of rough sketches outlining the scene sequence and major changes of action or plot in a production, such as a commercial or movie.) The storyboard should contain images as well as words.

4. Instruct writers to create a trailer for an imaginary movie and draw the major plot points or movie highlights on each of the five panels. (Writers may need 15 minutes or longer for this step.)

5. Have writers share their movie trailers with the whole group.

Ideas and Notes:

Stories in the Paper

Experiment:

Writers use the newspaper to come up with ideas for writing a scene.

Goal:

Learn the importance of internal or external conflict when telling a story.

Materials:

Several newspapers.

Experiment Steps:

1. Break into groups of three to five people.

2. Hand out sections of newspapers around the room.

3. From the newspaper, each group finds three story ideas that combine goal and conflict. This means that there must be some kind of problem for the characters in the story, a problem that they will want to overcome, and conflicting motivations or goals to make it harder to solve the problem.

4. Ask each group to select one of the story ideas to focus upon.

5. Ask writers to flesh out at least two of the characters, thinking about their motivations and goals, their backgrounds, their likes and dislikes.

6. Then, start writing the scene with dialogue and action, making sure not to directly state the motivation of each character, but to show it indirectly.

Ideas and Notes:

FICTION
EXPERIMENTS

A few words from fiction expert Katherine Taylor:

Katherine Taylor has won a Pushcart Prize, the McGinnis-Ritchie Award in fiction, and two Columbia University writing fellowships. Her stories have appeared in such journals as *Ploughshares*, *The Southwest Review*, and *Shenandoah*. Her first novel, *Rules For Saying Goodbye*, was published in spring 2007 by Farrar, Straus and Giroux.

What exactly is fiction? What makes it different from other genres?

I always say the difference between fiction and nonfiction is that fiction is a bunch of lies. I am an incorrigible exaggerator, and in fiction I get to exaggerate for a living.

What are the special components of fiction?

Fiction is a series of dialogues and situations. It's the imaginary people in your imaginary world moving through time and space, overcoming barriers, and making and destroying and repairing the relationships they have with each other.

How did you get into fiction?

Fiction chooses you. I have tried to write nonfiction, but I can't help editorializing and exaggerating, and we all know how those situations work out. Not well.

What sort of writing habits/schedule do you keep?

I write all day, every day. Sometimes this means I spend an entire day writing a letter, or an entire day sending emails, or an entire day working on a story that goes nowhere. I spend a lot of time making tea and cleaning the kitchen and trying to think of other things that will take me away from my desk, but most of the time, I'm at my desk from 7 a.m. until 7 p.m. I haven't always had this luxury. For many years I bartended or had very low-paying jobs in production, and then I would write in the car, on the subway, late at night, or anywhere I could steal a few moments of time.

Where do you look for inspiration?

I look for inspiration largely from my own life and, when my own life is not interesting enough to me, from the newspapers.

Do you just make everything up or is some of it true?
Where is the line between fiction and nonfiction?

I think the moment you start lying or exaggerating something that was true, it becomes fiction. This line between fiction and nonfiction is blurred by what we call memoir, which by definition, is reality as it's remembered in a first-person subjective narrative. Who's to say truth matters when what one remembers isn't exactly the truth? I stay away from this problem by calling everything fiction – fiction inspired by real life.

How would you recommend we get started writing a fiction piece?

Put two people in a room, or on someone else's patio, or waiting in a line together, or at a boring party, or (one of my personal favorites) in a car, and see what happens to them. This may not always be where you find the beginning of your piece – maybe the situation that arises comes somewhere in the middle, but it's a good place to start writing: in the middle of the action. I always try to start in the middle of the action. It gives a story energy.

What do you wish you would have known when you first started writing fiction?

I wish I would have known what a long, hard road it was going to be. On the other hand, if I had known all this, I may not have had the courage to pursue it.

Reading is a big part of writing. Can you suggest a few fiction writers for us to read?

Joan Didion, Ernest Hemingway, and John Cheever are three essential American writers. The Italian writer Italo Calvino strings together some of the most beautiful sentences in any language. Recently, I have been devouring Chekhov, and it's helped my writing and storytelling immensely. There's a subtlety to his humor and a sadness to even his most uplifting stories that I find very compelling.

When it comes to fiction...

Always:

Abandon yourself to the story. Write as if everyone you know, everyone you love and anyone who might have an opinion is dead. You can't write a story with other people's voices in your head. The famous writing teacher Gordon Lish said to his class one dispiriting day, when he felt the work up for discussion was particularly bad, "What is wrong with you people? Are you all waiting for your parents to die?" To write a good story, you must forget that anyone else may ever read it or care that you wrote it.

Never:

Censor yourself or edit as you write. Put everything in now. Take everything out later.

Imaginary Friend

Experiment:
Use imagination to create fictional characters.

Goal:
Explore character development techniques, including memory, drawing, and focusing on specific details.

Experiment Steps:

1. Ask writers to remember an imaginary friend they had when they were younger, or give them a few minutes to invent an imaginary friend.

2. Have writers draw a picture of this friend, including as many details as possible about their appearance, such as what shoes they are wearing, what length of hair they have, and what they are carrying. (Keep this short. Give writers a five-minute time limit.)

3. In a paragraph, have writers describe their friend, including things that are not visible, such as how they smell or what their voices sound like. (Tip: It is helpful to brainstorm all the things you might want to know about a character that are not visual before giving them some time to write.)

4. Have writers then describe even more information about this character, such as where he/she lives, where he/she works, and what hobbies he/she enjoys.

Ideas and Notes:

Story by Numbers

Experiment:

Writers work together to develop a story.

Goal:

Create a fictional story collaboratively.

Materials:

Posters, markers, one book (any book).

Setup:

Select an opening line at random from any available book, preferably a provocative line that would inspire the imagination as to what might happen next. Create a poster with that opening line at the top.

Experiment steps:

1. Give every writer a number, in sequence.

2. Explain the guidelines:

   - Each person will write one sentence on the poster to move a story forward, in order of their numbers.

   - Each new sentence must use at least one word from the previous sentence (this helps prevent people from thinking about their sentences ahead of time).

   - The story can be imaginative, but it must make sense.

   - Discuss basic storytelling elements, such as ensuring a story has a beginning, middle, and end, and that many powerful stories are about a specific character who discovers something or transforms in some way.

3. Call up each writer to the poster, giving them a 30-second time limit to think about and write their sentence.

4. After one round, the story can continue by going through the numbering cycle again.

5. Have one writer, or several writers, read the story aloud.

Ideas and Notes:

A Character is Born

Experiment:

Use different adjectives and points of view to create a fictional character.

Goal:

Show writers how to build a complex character.

Experiment Steps:

1. Ask writers to come up with six adjectives, including three physical and three non-physical adjectives, that might describe a character.

2. Ask writers to create a paragraph describing this character in a way that shows what he or she does without actually using any of the adjective words. For example, instead of the adjective "smart," you could write, "If you gave her your phone number once, she would remember it."

3. Now change the point of view. Ask writers to describe this character from another character's point of view, such as the character's mother or best friend, also without using the adjectives listed in step 1.

Ideas and Notes:

JOURNAL WRITING

A few words from journal writing expert Keren Taylor:

Keren Taylor is an arts educator, poet, singer/songwriter, and visual artist. She is the founder and executive director of WriteGirl, a creative writing and mentoring organization for teen girls in Los Angeles. Passionate about inspiring creativity, Keren has conducted hundreds of songwriting, poetry ,and Art & Words workshops in New York and Los Angeles for both children and adults. Her poetry appears in *So Luminous the Wildflowers – An Anthology of California Poetry* (Tebot Bach Press), *The San Gabriel Valley Poetry Review,* and *Wavelength*. She has performed her original music across the country in concert halls, theatres, clubs, and festivals. Her artwork has been exhibited at the Barnsdall Art Center, Rock Rose Art Gallery, and Gallery 727, and is displayed in personal collections. Keren holds a Bachelor of Arts degree in international relations from the University of British Columbia, a piano performance degree from the Royal Conservatory of Music in Toronto, and a diploma from the American Music and Dramatic Academy, New York City.

What is journal writing? What makes it different from other genres?

Keeping a personal writing journal has limitless possibilities. It can be a place for complete freedom of expression in both content and style. You can describe memories, family members, journeys, nature, events, goals, dreams, friends, purely imaginative stories, and more, or choose to keep a separate journal for each category. You can paint, draw, glue things inside, cut or fold the pages, press flowers or wrappers between the pages, or tape things inside, like fortune cookie fortunes or headlines from a newspaper. It's a fantastic place to play and create without constraints.

I thought journal writing is like writing in a diary. Is journal writing always private?

A journal can be a private place for self-expression, an art-and-words book to freely share with others, or a workout space to brainstorm and plan ideas for works of writing. It's a personal choice to make or to allow to unfold.

How did you get into journal writing? Did you choose it or did it choose you?

Writing has always been an activity that I've been drawn to, especially in times of high emotion, negative or positive. I write on anything handy if I don't have my journal, and then tape it in my journal later. Recently, I was in a restaurant and wanted to draft a letter to a friend, but they only had black cocktail napkins, so I wrote in the margins of a menu. Looking over the letter, I saw how the choppy wording of the Asian menu items changed my writing style – my sentences were short and abrupt. That was a fun discovery.

How often do you journal?

Not often enough. I would like to make time to write more in my journal. I have a very challenging job, running WriteGirl, so I write emails and proposals all day long. Sometimes it is hard for me to switch gears and allow myself to write anything I feel like writing. For a workaholic like me, it can feel like a waste of time at first. But every time I just let go and write, I learn something new or I get a new window to look inside myself, or I just find some release of an emotion I wasn't acknowledging.

How do you pick what to write about? Where do you look for inspiration?

For me, the best way to choose what to write about is to start right here, right now, with whatever is in front of me or on my mind. I might look out the window and start writing about what I see, or I will write about how I feel right now and what it feels like in my body. I also love to think about something in nature that I have experienced and use that as a jumping-off point. I found a very long white bird feather yesterday, and I know there are a few hundred words I need to write about that.

How would you recommend we get started writing a journal?

First of all, select a journal that you are drawn to. It could be the cover, the shape, the feel or look of the pages…but it really helps to have a book that you like right from the start. Then select a pen that you enjoy writing with. Next, it is important to find a comfortable, well-lit place to write. These may sound like insignificant details, but for me, they make a huge difference as to how often I write and how relaxed I am with my writing. As for content, one of the easiest ways to begin is to just start by writing about what you see, feel, smell, or observe around you right now. Another great way to start is just by writing, "I remember…" and then keep going on anything that comes up. In the spirit of freedom, I recommend writing upside down or in a circle or from the bottom of the page up – just approaching the page in an unconventional way can help take the pressure off yourself and free you from worrying about writing something "good."

Reading is a big part of writing. Can you recommend any examples of published journal writing for us to read?

Oh, yes. There are some fabulous published journals that can be very inspiring to pre through. Frida Kahlo's journal is a wonderful journey into her mind and artwork. The late photojournalist Daniel Eldon's journal is an amazing catalog of his travels in more than 40 countries. And I love the journals of Sabrina Ward Harrison – they are filled with colorful collages, writing, photographs, and drawings.

When it comes to journal writing…

Always:

Trust your instincts. Even if it feels silly or wrong or trite or boring, write whatever comes to you and give your creative spirit a chance to take over from your logical mind.

Never:

Edit yourself or judge yourself. Just write and go with your flow.

Personalize Your Journal

Experiment:

Decorate journals with colorful pictures, words, and materials.

Goal:

Make your journal reflect your unique identity.

Materials:

One journal for each writer; a collection of colorful art supplies such as a glitter pen, glitter glue, stickers, glue stick, stencils, and markers; random words and pictures cut from magazines; baskets or containers to hold and separate everything on the tabletop and plastic tablecloths to protect the table from any spills.

Experiment Steps:

1. Ask writers to think about the kinds of colors, animals, shapes, and words that they love. Ask them to think about the way they view themselves and how they might describe themselves to others.

2. Give writers a few minutes to browse the items on the table to see what they might want to use on the cover of their journals, as an expression of themselves or some part of themselves.

3. Give writers 15 to 20 minutes to create personalized journal covers using the materials on the table.

4. Ask writers to present their covers to the group, explaining their choices of colors, pictures, and words.

Ideas and Notes:

Candy-Coded Questions

Experiment:

Use a candy drawing to create a playful environment for writing about identity.

Goal:

Inspire writers to describe themselves and significant life moments.

Materials:

Posters, markers, and a collection of individually wrapped pieces of candy inside a covered jar or box. The candy wrappers need to be 4 different colors.

Setup:

1. Prepare posters, each with one of the four following prompts:

   - What if the next page of your journal was a door?
     Where would it take you?

   - Describe your scariest moment.

   - Describe someone who's influenced you.

   - Describe the last time you laughed really hard. (What was it about?)

2. Color-code the posters so that they match one of the four colors of the candy, either by using a poster or marker of the same color, or by taping a sample piece of candy to the corresponding poster.

Experiment Steps:

1. Writers select a piece of candy, unseen, from the covered jar or box.

2. Based on the color of the candy wrapper, writer refers to the corresponding poster and writes his or her response in his or her journal.

3. Writers can eat their selected candy!

4. Repeat steps 1 through 3.

5. Have writers share their writing with the group.

Ideas and Notes:

Shhhh – Don't Tell

Experiment:
Create a box of secrets, both real and imaginary, and use them to inspire stories.

Goal:
Have fun sharing a secret and use other people's secrets to reveal
something about your own life.

Materials:
A box, such as shoe box, with a hole in the top large enough for a hand.
Small pieces of blank paper equal to twice the number of writers participating.

Experiment Steps:

1. Ask writers to invent imaginary secrets (e.g., "When I was a kid, I ate a can of dog food";
   "I forgot to feed my turtle and it died"; "I broke my little brother's Shuffle").
   If necessary, give them guidelines for appropriateness of content.

2. Ask writers to write each secret on a small piece of paper, fold it, and place it in the box.

3. Each writer picks a secret out of the box and has seven minutes to write about it. Ask
   writers if it makes them think about their own secrets. Encourage them to write about
   absolutely anything that the secret makes them think about, but it should be something
   that really happened to them.

4. Repeat steps 1 through 3, but this time, ask writers to write their own real secrets.
   (If a writer picks his/her own, have him/her put it back!)

5. Ask writers to share their writing with the group.

Variation:
Instead of asking writers to write about their own lives, this can also be used as
a fiction experiment, where the secrets are used as prompts for fictional stories.

Ideas and Notes:

Beginnings

Experiment:

Create a unique and personal "first page," inspired by famous people who kept personal journals.

Goal:

Encourage writers to value themselves and their journals.

Materials:

A collection of first pages from journals to demonstrate as examples, copied from books and either tacked on a wall, distributed, or read to the group. Diaries to choose from might include George Washington, Frida Kahlo, Anne Frank, and Kurt Cobain.

Experiment Steps:

1. Give writers a few moments to read some samples of first pages from journals.

2. Present writers with the following choices:

Choice #1:

What do you want your journal to tell you each time you open it (a word, an image, a quote, a paragraph, etc.)? Write that word, quote, or paragraph (or draw that image) so you will see and be reminded of it every time you open your journal.

Choice #2:

Who or what is your journal (a feeling, an animal, a person, a place, etc.)? Let the journal tell you what it is.

3. Give writers 10 to 15 minutes to create their first page.

Ideas and Notes:

Come to Your Senses

Experiment:

Use another sense besides sight to tell a personal story.

Goal:

Explore all senses when writing a journal entry.

Materials:

Scented candles (without labels), different-shaped objects in a dark-colored bag, an MP3 device with headphones, and a CD of unusual music (something instrumental or something without English lyrics can be the most provocative).

Setup:

Set up a table with the various sense stations. Label a place card "Smell" with the candles; "Touch" with the bag; "Sound" with the ipod and headphones.

Experiment Steps:

1. Ask writers, in groups of three, to approach the table and experience one of the sense stations. Each group of three should be given only 15 seconds.

2. As writers return to their seats, ask them to begin writing about anything that the smell, texture, or sounds made them think about. Ask the writers to not allow their pens to stop once they start. Have them write, write, write!

3. Have writers share their writing with the group.

Variation:

Break this into three different experiments, focusing on one sense at a time – smell, touch, and sound. For example, instead of having the scents, textures, and music on a separate table, you can pass the candles around the room, then have them write, or play the music for the whole group, then write.

Ideas and Notes:

Running with a Pen

Experiment:

Write on posters around the room.

Goal:

Get writers out of their seats and help them discover how to use concrete details in their writing.

Materials:

Posters, markers.

Setup:

Write each question or prompt on top of each poster and leave a lot of space under it for several writers to fill in.

Choose some or all of the following questions prrompts for each poster:

- "You may quote me."
  Make up a quote for which you would want to be known.

- "Which literary character do you relate to and why?"

- Complete this sentence: "I wish… "

- "Finish my sentence."
  Some writers begin sentences and other writers complete them.
  (Draw a line vertically down the center to split the poster in two.)

- "What was the first thought you had when you woke up this morning?"

- "What was the first thing you noticed when you walked into the building?"

- "What was the first CD you owned?"

- "Describe your first day of school this year."

- Complete this sentence: "A writer needs a pen, paper and…"

Experiment Steps:

1. Encourage writers to focus on providing strong details as they move quickly around the room, writing on all the posters in fifteen minutes.

2. Have one writer read each poster out loud so everyone can share in the responses.

Ideas and Notes:

Fortune Cookie Wisdom

Experiment:

Partners write what they are thinking after reading the same fortune, from a fortune cookie.

Goal:

Discover that each person has something valuable to express despite seeing the world differently.

Materials:

Enough fortune cookies for half of the class (they will each share a cookie).

Experiment Steps:

1. Pair writers up.

2. Give each pair a cookie and ask them to break the cookie in half, sharing it as one reads the fortune and passes it on to the other writer.

3. After a couple of minutes, ask everyone to answer this question in their journal: What does this fortune make you think about?

4. Have them write continuously for five minutes.

5. Ask writers to share what they've written with their partners.

Ideas and Notes:

Our Hands — The Stories of Our Lives

Experiment:

Every hand is totally different. We all have markings and scars on our bodies that tell something about our lives. Writers will look at their hands to remember their stories.

Goal:

Recall an experience that might otherwise be forgotten and see that we carry our stories with us, on our bodies — stories are everywhere.

Materials (optional):

Magnifying glasses. Photocopier.

Experiment Steps:

1. Writers should take a moment to look at their hands closely: notice any marks, scars, or lines that they see. If you have brought magnifying glasses, get the students to pass them around and examine their hands even more closely. If you have access to a photocopy machine, have each writer photocopy their own hands.

2. Ask writers to describe their observations; often, these observations will lead them to a significant moment, memory, or experience they might not otherwise recall.

3. Have writers share their observations and writing with the group.

Ideas and Notes:

POETRY
EXPERIMENTS

Marlys West received her MFA from the Michener Center in Austin, Texas. The University of Akron Press published her book of poems, *Notes for a Late-Blooming Martyr,* in 1999. Her work has been published in many journals, newspapers, and anthologies. She was a Hodder Fellow at Princeton University and a National Endowment for the Arts grant recipient in poetry.

What is poetry? What makes it important or special?

I had to look this up online because when I started to answer, I realized everything sounded so overly dramatic: POETRY IS LIFE AND DEATH! POETRY IS EVERYTHING AND NOTHING! Poetry is the means by which I articulate that which is an unformed blob in my head!

Also, from Miriam-Webster's online dictionary: "writing that formulates a concentrated imaginative awareness of experience in language chosen and arranged to create a specific emotional response through meaning, sound, and rhythm."

So I could have said, "poetry is what I do," but so much of what I do isn't poetry (the cooking, the cleaning, the diaper changing, etc.) but then so much of that world DOES seem to end up in the poems, images or feelings or insights from the mundane (and therefore not at all mundane) world.

How did you get into poetry?

I think it was nursery rhymes, Dr. Seuss, and old fairy tales that laid the groundwork for my own work in poetry, but it took a very long time before I began reading and writing poetry regularly; so I wouldn't say that poetry chose me, but that I chose it, or found that I liked it better than I liked other pursuits: drawing, painting, cooking, baking, etc., that could have been as compelling.

If you were a lobbyist for poetry and poetry was about to be voted off the face of the earth, what argument would you make for the genre?

I would write a long list of things that must be voted off the face of the earth before we got to any of the art forms and I would write the list in verse form so that readers were not only persuaded by my wisdom in choosing; say, poverty and starvation before poetry, but were entertained and enlightened as well.

Where do you look for inspiration?

I look everywhere: my house, my family, my yard, my dictionary, my friends, my kitchen, my past, everywhere. I think that it's not the things that inspire me, but something else, an idea or thought that is running around in my head that gets linked to the outside images I'm collecting. That makes it sound like I'm a bug collector, doesn't it?

How would you recommend we get started writing a poem?

I think getting started is the hardest part, so I recommend leaping onto the page with any old phrase or sentence or thought and going from there. If I wait until I have the perfect image or words or idea, I'll be waiting until I'm a very old lady, so I tend to dive in, to write heaps of good, fun garbage and then edit, edit, edit, edit until the thing that was glimmering begins to shine. Then I edit more. I love editing. You don't have to get things right the first, second, or third time. You just keep going and it seems to come out all right, miraculously enough.

What do you wish you would have known when you first started writing poetry?

I wish I'd started sooner, but I was a bit intimidated by poetry in high school. We didn't read much of it and what we did read wasn't the best and most interesting poetry that a high school girl like me should read. I thought it was stupid and boring and I'm very sorry
I didn't know better, but I didn't.

Reading is a big part of writing. In addition to yourself, can you name a few poets for us to read?

I seem to read mostly modern, English-speaking poets, so I'm not a very eclectic source for a reading list, but that said, I think you should look at Lucille Clifton, who is amazing and lovely. I think you might look at Kay Ryan and Ai, too, who do very interesting work. Paul Muldoon and Charles Simic are good. Currently, I'm determined to read all the Nobel-prize-winning poets.

When it comes to poetry...

Always be willing to edit if the poem needs it!

Never think that you need an advanced degree to write something worthwhile!

Color Infusion

Experiment:
Writers create a poem from a single color and a few words.

Goal:
Give writers another way to approach the blank page and immerse them in sensual stimulation to evoke ideas and emotions.

Materials:
Slips of colored paper; posters and markers.

Experiment Steps:

1. Distribute one slip of colored paper to each participant.

2. Ask writers to think about things that the color reminds them of, such as clothing, objects in their home, school or food items. Ask them how the color makes them feel.

3. Give writers 10 to 15 minutes to write and freely associate ideas and memories based on the color they are holding.

4. Lead a group discussion about poetic devices. Write them on a poster at the front of the room.

5. Ask the writers to develop their writing into a poem by incorporating one or more poetic devices from the poster, such as alliteration, repetition and assonance.

6. Ask writers to share their writing with the group. Have the group try to identify any poetic devices the writer uses.

Ideas and Notes:

Reflection Through Music

Experiment:

Use music to prompt memories and emotions.

Goal:

Help writers tap into their memories and emotions by playing evocative music.

Materials:

iPod, CDs of movie soundtracks.

Experiment Steps:

1. Play short segments of movie soundtracks, selecting pieces that are not familiar.

2. Ask writers to listen to the rhythm, tone, mood, and feeling of the music and think of a family member or a family moment.

3. Ask writers to write about a family member or family moment and write in the same rhythm, tone, and mood of the music. Encourage writers to write words and phrases, not necessarily complete sentences.

4. Have writers share their writing with the group.

Ideas and Notes:

Enrich Your Description

Experiment:

Explore the language we choose to use. Try out different types of language to describe the same thing.

Goal:

Expand our perspective on expression and description.

Materials:

A variety of ordinary objects, example, pencils, pennies etc.

Experiment Steps:

1. Have each writer select a normal household object from a table, box, or bag.

2. Ask writers to describe the object in very basic, ordinary language.

3. Have writers rewrite, exchanging boring words for descriptive and sensory nouns and verbs.

4. Have writers share both versions with the group.

Ideas and Notes:

Lucky Seven Word Lottery

Experiment:

Use seven random words to write a quick poem.

Goal:

Turn poetry into a game, making it fun and approachable.

Materials:

Index cards.

Experiment Steps:

1. Distribute seven index cards to each writer.

2. Writers think of seven random words, writing one word on each index card.

3. Ask everyone to exchange word cards with a partner.

4. Ask writers to create a poem about family or a family celebration using all seven words. Give writers a time limit, such as seven minutes, to keep it fast and fun.

5. Ask writers to share their poems with the group. After reading a poem, have the writer read out the seven words they incorporated.

Variation:

Select a different theme for a poem, such as what you love/hate about your neighborhood or a place in the world you would like to visit.

Ideas and Notes:

Family Portrait

Experiment:

Write and edit a poem in a group.

Goal:

Create spontaneous and collaborative poetry.

Materials:

Posters, markers.

Setup:

Write a lead-off line on several posters:

- The thing about my family is...

- One thing I love about my mother is…

- When I think of my father, I think of the smell of…

- When my family celebrates, what you hear is…

- In my family, I play the role of…

Experiment Steps:

1. Writers move around the room to write on the posters. Anyone may write a line on any poster, as long as it supports the first line.

2. Give writers a specific time limit, such as 10 minutes.

3. Give the completed posters to small groups of three to five writers each.

4. Each group constructs a poem using the lines written on their poster using the following guidelines:

- They may re-order the lines and omit lines.
- If they would like to add anything (words or complete lines), they can only use words that are already written somewhere on the poster.

5. Ask writers to write their new poem on a blank poster.

6. Display posters of the new poems for the whole group to read.

Ideas and Notes:

Questions and Objects

Experiment:

Write a poem based on interaction with objects and the ideas, images or stories they evoke.

Goal:

Learn how questions can be effective and evocative in a poem.

Materials:

A big box full of odd objects, such as a classroom's lost and found collection. Or ask each writer to bring in something unusual from home. Find an example of a poem filled with questions, such as a section of Pablo Neruda's poem, *The Book of Questions*.

Experiment Steps:

1. Hand out the sample poem and discuss.

2. Ask writers to choose an object randomly from a bag.

3. Ask writers to examine the object using as many of their senses as possible.

4. Have writers describe not only what they see, but also what emotions these objects invoke. Encourage each writer to start each stanza with a question.

5. Ask writers to edit their writing to eliminate inactive words.

6. Have writers read poems aloud, showing the group their object after they've read the poem.

Ideas and Notes:

Accordion Poems

Experiment:
Working in small groups, writers create poems.

Goal:
Release the need to write in logical or chronological order.

Materials:
Blank sheets of paper – enough for one page per group.

Experiment Steps:

1. Organize writers in groups of 5 to 8 people, and hand out paper for each pair.

2. Each group decides on a theme for their poem, using something that happened to them in the past six months.

3. One person writes the first two lines (can be a phrase or a sentence) of poetry, folding over the first line so that the next person can only read the second line.

4. Keeping the theme in mind, the next person writes a line and then folds the paper again so only the line they just wrote is visible.

5. Repeat, until there is no more room on the paper.

6. Unfold the paper, which will resemble an accordion, with all the folds now unfolded.

7. Have groups share their poems out loud with the group, also announcing the theme of their poem.

Ideas and Notes:

SONGWRITING
EXPERIMENTS

A few words with songwriting expert Michelle Lewis:

Michelle Lewis's career as a songwriter began ten years ago, when, as an artist signed to Giant Records, the more commercial songs she wrote for her albums began to get covered by a diverse number of artists (Kelly Osbourne, Amy Grant, Cher). She soon decided that there was more dignity in writing songs for other people than there was in schlepping around the country in a van and moved to Los Angeles (from her native NYC) to begin writing songs full-time. From her own experience as an artist, she brings a highly credible and creative touch to her writing with, and for, others (Fefe Dobson, Lindsay Lohan, Michelle Branch, Courtney Jaye). She is also currently developing a kid's TV show for *Playhouse Disney*, managing the band *Shut Up Stella*, and recording with her band, The Dilettantes.

What exactly is songwriting? Do you have to be able to play an instrument?

In the most basic sense, writing songs is putting words to music.

You don't have to play an instrument to write lyrics or compose a simple melody. I play guitar and piano, though, because it's like having a bigger vocabulary or a wider palette of colors to choose from.

What are the special components of songwriting?
What makes it different from other genres like poetry?

There is an alchemy involved in songwriting that goes beyond its components - lyrics, rhythm, and melody - which can make a song both memorable and emotionally compelling.

Lyric writing is different from poetry because the sounds and rhythms of the words are as important as their meanings. You want to use phrases and ideas that bear repeating. Also, lyricists keep the singer in mind…using words that "sing well" with open vowel sounds and not TOO many consonants or syllables.

How did you get into songwriting? (Did you choose it or did it choose you?)

Songwriting chose me. I was the daughter of two musicians, so I grew up completely surrounded by music. Although I went to college to study medicine, I ended up playing in rock bands all four years. I began writing songs for one of those bands (because I got sick of playing covers) and got a publishing deal (like a book deal for songs) one year out of school. Needless to say, I scrapped the med school plans.

If you were a lobbyist for songwriting and songwriting was about to be voted off the face of the earth, what argument would you make for the genre?

I would say that you could TRY to vote songs off the face of the earth, but by their very nature they would still exist – in underground song speakeasies and on contraband records, in people's heads and sung to their kids at night. You know how a song gets in your head and just…won't…leave? It's because songs are so much more than words on a page! They represent time and place and emotions and memories. I'd say, vote away! It wouldn't matter; songwriting would go on.

What sort of writing habits/schedule do you keep and/or recommend?

My number one rule is NO TV DURING THE DAY!!! Even though I work from home, I don't turn on the TV (or read magazines or web surf) until all the writing is done.

My mind is the most clear in the morning, so before checking email or eating breakfast, I try to write down whatever ideas I had while I was waking up.

Which reminds me – leave a tape recorder or notebook and pen by your bed. If you think you'll still remember the idea later, believe me, you won't.

Change of scenery – when I'm stuck, I move. I leave the room, go for a walk, take the laptop to Starbucks, etc. Meeting a friend for lunch or a mani/pedi is not the same thing. That's more like taking a break (which is fine, too)

Dare to suck. A very successful songwriter friend of mine says that whenever we're writing, she can tell I'm censoring an idea. She'll see me thinking a little too hard and say, "Come on, Michelle, dare to suck!" It's just a natural part of the brainstorming process. Sometimes your most ridiculous idea will inspire something really good in someone else, or at least inspire a good laugh.

Where do you look for inspiration?

Other songs I love.
The natural rhythm in things around me – windshield wipers, walking, a phrase, etc.
My dog.
Book titles.
Conversations.

How would you recommend we get started writing a song?

Look for the natural rhythm and melody in everyday phrases and words.

When you find some you like, repeat them - over and over.

When you've settled in on a constant rhythm for the phrase, make up another line that rhymes with it.

Try adding some melody to your phrases and sing them out loud.

Think about how little kids are always singing. Ssometimes it's a song they know and sometimes they just make something up. Make something up!

What do you wish you would have known when you first started writing songwriting?

That I didn't have to write ALL my ideas in one song! That I'd have plenty of ideas left for plenty of other songs. That songs are not so precious – you can always write another one.

When it comes to songwriting…

Always:
Start with an idea that bears repeating.
Sing your idea out loud!
Remember that simple is better.

Never:
Use the word "squelch" in lyrics – or words that start with "squ" in general – or use words with too many syllables, like "paleontology" – that would just be silly. Never worry too much about making sense.

Anything else we need to know?

Songwriting is part "art" and part "craft." The art part is the inspiration, the beautiful melody or the profound idea you have. The craft part is something you learn over time: Where does a pre-chorus go? Is this song too long? Do the verses tell enough of a story?

Oh, and every rule I've learned and used in songwriting, I've also broken.

Universal Song Themes

Experiment:

By listening to music, identify the kinds of themes often found in pop songs.

Goal:

Highlight the emotional motivations behind most song lyrics and get writers
to start writing in the short, casual style of pop lyrics.

Materials:

One blank poster; boom box or stereo; a selection of five songs. It can be challenging
to find contemporary pop songs that do not contain profanity or explicit lyrics.
We recommend reviewing the full lyrics of songs on the web before playing the song
to the writers. Some recommended artists to consider: India Arie, Aretha Franklin,
The Supremes, The Beatles.

Setup:

Put a poster on the wall with the heading, "What are themes that we hear?" (Note
to leader: Some common themes in songs include: celebration of love, expression
of happiness, breakup of a relationship, expression of loneliness, declaration of self-
empowerment or strength, anger/frustration toward someone, etc.)

Experiment Steps:

1. Play a portion of one of the songs (about 1 minute is usually enough). Ask writers to focus
   on the lyrics and write down what they think is the theme of the song. Let them know
   that there can be more than one theme in a song, and that a theme can be one word
   (sadness), or it can be a phrase (leaving a relationship). You may need to play more of the
   song if writers aren't sure.

2. Ask writers to share the themes they wrote with the group.
   Write their responses on the poster.

3. Repeat Steps 1 and 2 with four more songs.

4. Ask writers to select one of the themes on the poster that is something they can identify
   with, and start brainstorming a title and some words and phrases on that theme. It is
   important that they do NOT write in paragraph form. It might be helpful to give writers
   some specific limiting parameters, such as, "write only five-word phrases on this theme"
   or "write a two-word phrase
   on this theme, then write a three-word phrase, then four, etc."

5. Have writers share their theme and some of the phrases they wrote.

Ideas and Notes:

Songs About Me

Experiment:
Create titles for songs that describe aspects of your life.

Goal:
Begin thinking about universal song concepts.

Materials (optional):
Billboard Magazine song charts listing the top current songs.
(Available online and at newsstands.)

Experiment Steps:

1. Discuss song titles. Ask writers what the titles are of some of the songs they love. Discuss what makes for a strong song title. (Titles are often short – usually one-to-five words. They quickly convey the whole meaning of the song and they are often imperative or declarative.)

2. Ask writers to brainstorm song titles for a song about some aspect of their lives. Use any or all of the suggestions below. We have included some examples.

   What would be the TITLE for a song...

   ...about your family?

   ...about your worst or best day last week? ("The Math Test Blues")

   ...about the last person who broke your heart? ("Go Away!")

   ...about something you dream of? ("If I Was a Rich Girl")

   ...about someone you have a crush on? ("If You Only Knew")

   ...about the last argument you had? ("I Told You So!")

   ...about something you love to do? ("Ice Cream Serenade" or "Dancing in the Dark")

   ...what is the title of your personal theme song? ("I Will Survive" or "R-E-S-P-E-C-T")

3. Read out the categories again and encourage writers to shout out their song titles.

Ideas and Notes:

Chorus Lines

Experiment:

Write the chorus of a song.

Goal:

Give writers an understanding of traditional rhyming patterns in song lyrics.

Materials:

Boom box or stereo; song to play; lyrics of the song to hand out.

Setup:

Select a song to play for the group, and photocopy lyric sheets so everyone can read along. A few suggested songs: "Lean On Me," "I Will Survive," "Let it Be," "We Will Rock You/We are the Champions," "Every Breath You Take."

Experiment Steps:

1. Hand out the lyrics to a song.

2. Play one section of that song (ideally, the chorus or the most recognizable part of the song), focusing on only four or eight lines. It might be helpful to ask writers to focus only on the rhyming structure as they listen, not to whether or not they like or know the song. Ask writers to underline the words that rhyme.

3. Play the section of song again and clearly point out the rhyming lines.

4. Play the section of song one more time, this time asking writers to listen to the rhythm of the words. Help the writers count the number of syllables in the selected lines.

5. Ask writers to write their own lyrics to that section of the song, matching the form of the song by keeping the same number of syllables and the rhyming scheme. Encourage writers to change the theme or content of their lyrics, such as writing about the opposite emotional theme than what is in the song.

6. Have writers share their lyrics with the group.

Variation:

Have writers write completely new lyrics to an entire song that you hand out to them, without hearing the song at all, keeping the same syllable count/rhythm and rhyming scheme.

Ideas and Notes:

This One's for You

Experiment:

Write song lyrics within a specific meter and rhyming pattern.

Goal:

Help writers turn their prose into song lyrics by giving them a specific form to follow.

Materials:

Sample lyrics with specific rhyme schemes, or short rhyming poems.

Experiment Steps:

1. Ask writers to make a list of people they love. It could be a friend, a girlfriend/ boyfriend, or a family member.

2. Then ask writers to select one person on their lists and write a letter to them, telling them exactly what they love about them. Have them include any questions that they might want to ask these people.

3. Hand out sample lyrics or poems. Read aloud and discuss the rhyming pattern.

4. Ask writers to rewrite a portion of the letter they wrote so that it fits into the rhyming and syllable structure of one of the sample lyrics or poems.

5. Ask writers to share their lyrics with the group.

Ideas and Notes:

PERSONAL ESSAY
WRITING
EXPERIMENTS

A few word from personal essay writing expert Allison Deegan:

For most of her career, Allison Deegan has been a business and marketing consultant and writer, specializing in new ventures and strategy. She's also a screenwriter. Currently, she's a business manager for the Los Angeles County Office of Education and recently earned her Doctorate in Education. Allison serves as WriteGirl's associate director, and has helped many of our girls with scholarship applications and, in the process, helped them achieve their dreams of entering top colleges around the country.

What is a personal essay?

It's a story about you, a piece that reveals enough important details to make the reader feel like they are there with you, experiencing what you experienced. Even though it's all about you, readers can relate it to their own lives.

Um…aren't essays what they make you write in school? What is so great about them?

The great thing about personal essays is you can capture a moment in time, write about what you learned, what you wish you'd known, how the things you've seen and done have made you the person you are today, and communicate that journey to everyone who reads your work. Essays are one part memory, one part advice, one part story, and one part entertainment, all wrapped up for the reader to breathe in. You get to know yourself better, and readers get to know you, too.

How did you get into personal essay writing?

Since WriteGirl started, our members have been inspired to write about their lives, sometimes using fiction, sometimes just the cold, hard truth, and sometimes a very intriguing combination of the two called "creative nonfiction." I've worked with many members who are in the middle of the college application challenge and have seen them struggle to craft the "perfect" essay. What I've learned is that, if they follow the WriteGirl way of telling their personal stories, a strongly voiced, entertaining, and engaging personal essay will emerge, perfect for just about any college application. My number one passion is getting kids started on the college journey, which will help them reach their potential. Often, that journey starts with a great essay!

What sort of writing habits/schedule do you keep?

I write every day, whether it's business writing, professional memos, creative pieces, long (very long!) emails and letters, or lists of things I want to write tomorrow. I have a busy schedule so I am never, ever without a pad and pen, just in case I have to wait in a line for 15 minutes or have an idea or line of dialogue that just can't wait until I get home. When I have a longer piece to complete, I turn off my phone and put on "white noise" music that fills the air and soothes me, but doesn't drown out the crazy characters who are talking inside my head.

Where do you look for inspiration or essay topics?

Every time I want to call a friend and tell them what just happened, I wonder if it could be an essay topic. If it's interesting enough to tell people you care about, it must say something important about you, and it might be intriguing to readers. I'm inspired when I connect strongly with an essay in a newspaper or magazine. I always think, "I know exactly how that feels," and wish I'd made the effort to write about it myself!

How would you recommend we get started writing an essay?

Make a list of the things, people, places, and/or experiences that have been important in your life. Select one of those things to tell a stranger, especially a stranger you really want to know you. That is a good essay topic to start with. Take a journalistic approach at first, conveying the facts, history, timeline, etc. Then go back and fill in the emotions, the observations, and the knowledge you gained about yourself or your world.

What do you wish you had known when you first started writing essays?

I wish I had known that other people are likely to feel how I feel about a lot of things, and that sharing it with readers is a powerful way of processing it for myself. I didn't know that there could be a sense of community derived from sharing my experiences with others. I didn't think my life was interesting enough! Now I know that if you're truthful and really care about connecting with your reader in an entertaining way (which doesn't have to mean being humorous), a good essay is nearly guaranteed.

Reading is a big part of writing. Can you name a few essayists/examples for us to read?

I read a lot of newspaper Op-Ed columnists. Sometimes their essays are very personal, sometimes they're about the world or politics, but the great ones always manage to give you their individual takes on any topic or situation. I'm a fan of Paul Krugman, Frank Rich and Maureen Dowd of the *New York Times,* and Steve Lopez and Al Martinez, who I read in the *Los Angeles Times. Newsweek* has a great personal essay column (right in the front of the magazine) called "My Turn," which offers all kinds of stories from around the country written by contributors.

When it comes to personal essays…

Always tell the truth as you see it, but make it entertaining. It's an essay, not a diary.

Write what you know, and then make it interesting for a reader who will never meet you.

Never be afraid to leave the first-person vantage point behind – inhabit a creative voice to tell a story you've experienced for real.

Anything else we need to know?

It may seem that the things you could write about have already been said and done. Don't give up – keep up a practice of making lists, taking notes, capturing impressions and observations, and when the time comes, you'll be practiced in the fine art of essay writing and have subject material to spare!

Vote for It

Experiment:
Writers read and vote on paragraphs excerpted from three different essays and talk about why they made their choices.

Goal:
Discover the emotional core that makes an essay successful.

Materials:
Three paragraphs from essays – a strong one from a former student, two from famous writers.

Experiment steps:

1. Read and distribute, with the authors' names omitted, three paragraphs from three different essays. One should be an excerpt from a strong essay by a former student and the other two should be from famous writers.

2. Give writers five minutes after each essay to write a short "review" of each one. It may be helpful to lead a discussion to give writers specific things to look for, such as the vocabulary the writer uses, the theme of the essay, the tone of voice the writer uses, etc.

3. Have writers vote about which paragraph they liked best.

4. Ask writers to explain why they made their choice, before revealing who wrote each of the essays.

Ideas and Notes:

Key Changes

Experiment:

Brainstorm to find out which experiences in your life you can draw on when writing a personal essay for a scholarship or college application essay.

Goal:

Find emotional experiences in your life to create powerful and detailed personal essays.

Materials:

Movie posters; pictures or books depicting teens in difficult situations; one key for each writer.

Experiment Steps:

1. Lead a discussion about teens in movies or books, including what challenges they faced, what they learned, and how they changed. Display posters, pictures, or books.

2. Ask writers to make a list of experiences or challenges from which they learned something about themselves, their families, communities, people in general, or the world. At this point, they should try to write as many as possible without giving too much detail. Examples might be something or someone that broke your heart, a point at which you went in a different direction, or a time when you found out something that was really important to you.

3. Give a key to each writer. Ask them to select one of the experiences on their list and write down the key thing they learned or action they took that allowed them to go through or overcome that challenge.

4. Ask writers to tell the whole story of that challenge or experience, giving all the details about who, what, where, when, and why it happened.

Ideas and Notes:

Show Off Your True Colors

Experiment:

Writers make a list of personal characteristics they want to reveal, pick one of these characteristics, and write about a personal experience that demonstrates this quality.

Goal:

Learn how to use strong details to demonstrate a main point and reveal personal character through experiential writing to form strong college admissions and scholarship essays.

Materials:

A variety of personal essays copied from newspapers or magazines.

Experiment Steps:

1. Leader hands out an assortment of essays for students to read.

2. The group brainstorms about personal characteristics that are demonstrated in the essays, writing a list of positive and negative qualities on the board.

3. Writers make a list of five personal characteristics that they want readers to know about them, using the list on the board or making up their own. These could be characteristics they're proud of, ones they've overcome, one that is evolving in them over time, or something they're still wrestling with.

4. Writers brainstorm about experiences that demonstrate these five characteristics.

5. Writers choose one of the characteristics and an experience that demonstrates it. They write about this experience, seeking to provide complete sensory details (sight, sound, smell, touch, taste) and to demonstrate the characteristic without saying what it is.

6. In pairs, writers exchange essays and try to identify what personal characteristic the other writer is trying to demonstrate. They tell each other what they think.

Ideas and Notes:

Stand Up for Essay Writing

Experiment:

Writers move around the room and ask each other personal essay questions. They answer each other, using one main point and one detail to demonstrate their main point.

Goal:

Learn how to support the main points of your essay with strong details.

Materials:

Index cards with opinion and descriptive essay questions on them. (Leader can prepare the cards or writers can write their own questions on the index cards from a list of prompts.)

Experiment Steps:

1. Have the whole group discuss one essay question and brainstorm some main points that might be included in that essay. Sample questions:

   - *What are the qualities of a good friend?*
     (kind, considerate, generous, interesting)

   - *Should uniforms be required at school?*
     ("Yes" reasons: kids do it anyway, to help behavior;
     "No" reasons: health risks, second-hand smoke, dirty).

2. Group brainstorms specific supporting details to support each of these points of the essay.

3. Give an index card to each writer.

4. Writers stand up and move around the room to talk with other people and get their help with their essay topic. Each person they approach must offer them one main point and a supporting detail. Writers can make up the details to make it more fun, but they should try to look for different types of details each time (a personal experience, a made-up statistic or study, a detailed example).

5. Have writers share their essay topics and details with the whole group.

Ideas and Notes:

ZIPPERS:

FAST WRITING EXPERIMENTS

TO DO AT A BUS STOP

OR AT THE BEACH

OR WAITING FOR THE

TOAST TO POP UP

Screenwriting Zippers:

1. Hard to Get

Think about how couples play hard to get and write down five different ways of showing or saying "I want you to love me" WITHOUT using the words or the actions that would most obviously go with those words.

2. Find the Voice

Great characters have what's called "voice" – they talk in a distinctive way that's true to where they're from, their background, education, culture, and most importantly, their own unique personality. Choose one of the examples below and write it as if it was being spoken by someone you know very well, such as your best friend or your mother. Take a moment to "hear" their voice in your head, then start to write.

   a. Tell a simple fairy tale, like the story of The Three Little Pigs.
   b. Give directions from your house to the grocery store.
   c. Choose a simple recipe and give the cooking instructions.
   d. Explain how to do an exercise or a dance move.

3. Talk to Yourself

Write a scene between you – and you. Choose yourself now and your 70-year-old self, or choose yourself now and your seven-year-old self.

4. Say that Again

Write a break-up scene. Now write the same scene, but change a significant detail about each character, such as where they are from, what kind of family they have, or what is special about them. If they are outgoing, make them shy – just change something – and see how that changes the way they speak.

5. Take Two

Take One: Put your character in front of a mirror practicing for an important moment – it could be asking a teacher to change a grade, asking a friend for an apology, or asking a crush out on a date. Write down what your character says.

Take Two: Now, put that aside and write the scene where your character is actually living that important moment. How does your scene compare to the practice session? How does it change the way the character talks?

6. Talk with Your Mouth

When you write a scene, what your characters DO can say as much as their words. Write a scene focusing on your characters' actions. Does a character simply turn away instead of answering a question? Start flipping channels on the TV to avoid a fight instead of just yelling? Punch a wall?

7. What I Wish I'd Said Was…

Go back to a moment in your life where you wish you'd said something different than what you actually did. Write a scene where the perfect words come out of your mouth…satisfaction at last!

8. Fish Out of Water

Think of a wacky, eccentric, or funny friend you have. Now imagine placing that friend in the exact OPPOSITE setting than that which he or she is accustomed to. (The movie term for this is "fish out of water.") Your friend has to interact with someone he or she would never normally talk to. Write the scene/conversation.

9. Odd Buddies

Think of two friends who have NOTHING in common. Now force them to do some activity together, like solve a crime or make a peanut butter sandwich. (The movie term for this is "buddy" or, if it's funny, "buddy comedy.")

10. Mistaken Identity

Imagine a character who is mistaken for someone else; the more outlandish, the more story possibilities, like your math teacher is mistaken for an international spy! (The movie term for this is, naturally, "mistaken identity.") Write the first scene of this movie, in which someone approaches the character, mistaking him or her for someone else.

11. Read a Screenplay

The best way to learn about screenwriting is to read screenplays! The links below will help you find lots of free screenplays on the Internet. (In some cases, you can find early drafts as well as the final "shooting" script. Even the pros have to rewrite!)

http://www.movie-page.com/movie_scripts.htm

http://www.script-o-rama.com/snazzy/dircut.html

http://www.joblo.com/moviescripts.php

http://www.dailyscript.com/links.html

Pick a scene from an early draft of a script and compare it to the same scene in the finished film. How is it the same? How is it different? Did anything surprise you in the writing of the scene? What elements of the scene do you think were dictated by the writer and what parts were the director's or the actors' contributions?

Creative Non-Fiction Zippers:

1. How to Make Me Happy

Write how someone can make you happy in three steps. Be specific, like spelling out exactly what kind of chocolate you want. (You can find examples of this experiment in the WriteGirl anthology, *Nothing Held Back*.)

2. The Scoop on Your Family

Write a paragraph about a family member you see often. Write about his/her day or his/her routine or simply how he or she is at the dinner table.

3. A Special Place

Write about a place that's important to your family (maybe your family goes to your grandmother's house every Sunday for dinner or to a favorite movie theater once a month), or pick somewhere in your neighborhood that's important to the community (maybe it's a church, a park, or a restaurant). Who else goes there? What do people talk about? How does it feel to be there? Pick a specific time you went there and focus on telling the story of what it is about this place that makes it special.

4. The History of Things

Pick an important object that is significant to your family or your culture or community and write a brief history of it. For example, this could be a dress that gets passed down for weddings, or a Halloween costume everyone in your family has worn at one time, a hat, a picture, a doll, a book, a recording of music, a Christmas ornament. Describe what it looks like, feels like, and/or sounds like. Explain what it's used for and when. How long has it been in the family or community? Why is it important? If you'd like, you can give the object a personality and/or a consciousness and let it tell its own story in its own voice. (You can find examples of "The Oldest Thing I Own" in the WriteGirl anthology, *Pieces of Me*.)

5. Not Just a Business

Pick a business that you walk or drive past every day. It may be a place you've been curious about or a place you've barely noticed. Interview the owner or manager about the company's history. See if you can find out its ties to the community or any information you think people would be surprised to know, and write about it.

6. Extra Ordinary

Pick one of the most ordinary things you do and write a personal essay about it. For instance, do you always burn the toast because someone else always pushes the knob over to the highest setting? Do you always check your teeth in the toaster while you're waiting for the toast? Get impatient and pop up the toast before it's done? What do you think about while you're waiting for the toast?

7. Mix N' Match

Find a way to put two of your interests together in one place. Think about two interests that might not normally go together. Should the local gym have an "All-You-Can-Eat" buffet? What would it be like for Adopt-A-Pet to team up with an online dating service? What would a Chocolate Film Festival be like?

8. Found Objects

Reach into your bag or your pocket. Pick an object you find there. Examine it carefully. You may see something new even if you've looked at it many times. Feel its texture. Smell it. Hold it up to the light. Then write about whatever it makes you think about. You might write directly about this object and what it means to you, or maybe you'll talk about how you came to have this object, or it may remind you of a related memory. It may tap into memories, dreams, and fears. Go there. Go where the object takes you.

9. Read All About It

Write about your life in headlines only. First, give your newspaper a name. Then, write the headlines of the first page of the newspaper.

10. Tell Them What You REALLY Think

There's someone you need to say something to. If you were to sit down and write them a letter right now, who would you write to? What do you want to tell this person? What is your intention in writing? You don't need to mail it, but definitely start writing now.

Journalism Zippers:

1. Celebrity Interviews

Look up the bio of someone famous online. Go to Google, type in the person's name and the word "bio" or "biography." Read the bio and think of questions you'd like to ask. Maybe there's a particular area you find interesting. Think of questions people don't normally ask. If you look online at the various interviews of this person, make sure none of your questions are the same. If the person has an email address, send one of your questions to him or her.

2. Profile Yourself

Write a paragraph about who you are; write it from the third-person (as if you were the journalist writing this story about someone else). Insert quotes and have fun with the details.

3. Pet Peeves

Make a list of things you don't like in your house (early curfew, noisy brothers and sisters, no television) and write an editorial about the things that frustrate you about your living situation. Try to keep your tone and style consistent, whether it's comedic, dramatic, or irritated.

4. Smile, You're on Camera

Journalism is capturing life in a snapshot. Pick something you'd like to observe. It could be your family at the dinner table, the traffic on your street, or people shopping in the local corner store. Take notes of what you see or record it so you can look back at it afterward. Use all of your senses: sight, smell, touch, taste, and hearing – to capture what is going on around you. Recreate the scene that you have witnessed as accurately as possible in a paragraph. Don't forget to use strong verbs and to incorporate quotes from conversations you heard.

5. Talk the Talk

The art of the interview is key for a reporter. Find an area in which your friend or family member is an expert and interview him/her about it. (Remember to let her ramble a bit —that leads to some good stuff.) If you have an older relative, you can type it up and give it to the extended family for a present.

6. Not!

Write an editorial expressing an opinion you passionately believe in. Now write it again, taking the opposite side. Your goal is to be every bit as passionate and convincing this time.

7. Don't See This Movie ... Or Do

Choose a movie, TV show, CD, or book and review it. Be careful not to give the whole thing away! Tell your readers why they should snatch it up, avoid it, or give it a shot if they have nothing better to do. Send it in an email to everyone you know or submit it to a community online paper.

Journal Writing Zippers:

1. Trash or Treasure?

Find a piece of paper in your pocket or backpack. It could be a receipt, a movie ticket stub, a wrapper, etc. Tape it onto a page in your journal. Write down what it says about you. Give all the details.

2. Let Music Inspire You

Put on some music (instrumental music so you won't be distracted by the lyrics) and use all your senses to continue the phrase, "I remember..." Feel free to start on a new memory when the music changes. (Tip: ask a friend to loan you one of his or her CDs – fresh, unfamiliar music is great for inspiration.)

3. A Letter in a Bottle

Write a letter to yourself in the future. It could be five years, ten years, or even thirty years from now. What would you like to tell yourself about how you are feeling now? If you want, stick it in something fun, like a bottle.

4. Break Your Patterns

Write with a different pen than you usually use, a crayon, or charcoal. Write in a spiral, upside-down, around the edges, over top of a picture, in HUGE letters, in tiny, tiny writing... see how your writing changes when you change things around.

5. NaNo Nano! Shazbot!

Make up your own language. Write out a code for what words = what and then write a journal entry with these new words.

6. I am a Goldfish

Imagine waking up in the morning as a kind of animal. What kind of animal are you? Write a story about your day as you go about your normal activities as this animal, and show how your family and friends react.

7. I See a Dark Stranger In Your Future...

Pretend you are a fortune teller or psychic. Imagine you are coming to yourself for a reading. Write down what you would tell yourself about your past, your present, and your future in all areas of your life (spiritual, school, finances, love, etc). Feel free to make stuff up about the planets and the stars if you don't know anything about astrology.

8. Two of You?

You're going to be cloned. Write a list of helpful hints for your clone, knowing what you know about yourself.

9. Dear Prudence

Sometimes people start journal entries with "Dear Diary." Try starting off a journal entry with "Dear somebody." You choose. It can be somebody fictional or real:

a relative, a friend, an imaginary friend you had when you were three, somebody famous (living or dead), etc.

10. He Said, She Said...

Try writing about a day in your life in the third-person; for example: "She woke up in a great mood, but it all went downhill when..."

11. When I'm Fifty-Four...

Write a letter to go in a time capsule that you're going to open when you're fifty-four (or some other age). Tell your fifty-four-year-old self every single thing you want to remember about being the age you are right now.

12. My Planet

Pretend a planet has been made to order just for you. What's the vegetation like? The animal life? The atmosphere? How much water? What's the weather like? How do the people live? Or are you the only person?

13. What's In a Name?

Write about your name: first name, last name, middle name, nickname, names you were almost called, names you wish you were or weren't called, etc. We all have powerful feelings about our names.

14. Go with the Flow

Brainstorm: open up your journal and write down everything that comes to your mind for the next five minutes. You might find yourself continually jumping to new thoughts, or you might find that there's one topic on your mind that is compelling you. Keep your pen going.

15. It Feels Like the First Time

First experiences almost always produce powerful memories. Write about a first experience. Here are some possibilities, but almost any first experience will work: The first time you (lost, won, felt embarrassed), your first trip, summer camp, day of school, best friend, kiss, shock, etc.

16. Smell It

The sense of smell is the most powerful sense to evoke memories. Think of one smell, the first that pops into your head, and write about a memory that goes with it.

17. Cave Walls

Imagine that your journal is the wall of a prehistoric cave. Write a journal entry describing your day, but instead of writing words, use drawings and symbols to tell the story.

18. Yesterday and Tomorrow

Write a page about yesterday and then write a page about tomorrow.

Fiction Zippers:

1. Go out for Lunch

Create a character, considering likes, dislikes, personality, and appearance. This main character invites you to lunch. You don't know your character very well, but you accept the invitation. Write what happens during your lunch. Try to get to know the character better. What does he/she say? What is ordered? What do you talk about?

2. Pull out the Gloves

Think of a major fight you have had with someone or make one up. Remember the details of it and then write it as a scene from the other person's point of view. What emotions would have prompted them to act and talk as they did?

3. Fairy Tale Mutations

Continue the story of your favorite or least-favorite fairy tale.

4. An Eavesdropper on Your Life

Write a scene about an important event in your life but write it as someone who is watching you. See if you can describe the emotions you were feeling with your actions and words.

5. Random Stranger

Pick a random stranger you see on the street or in a store and create a history about them. Where did they just come from? Where are they going? Why are they there at that moment?

6. I Am Sam

Try writing a journal entry as if you are someone else - maybe the guy sitting a few tables away at the coffee shop where you write, a character from a story you're working on, or the president, your best friend, your worst enemy, a teacher, your favorite author while he or she was writing your favorite book, your favorite athlete before a big game.

7. Who's Your Muse?

In Greek mythology, there are four muses who inspire poets: Erato covers love poetry, Thalia's in charge of playful poetry, Polyhymia's territory is sacred poetry, and Calliope's is epic poetry. Create a muse for yourself. Describe him or her (or it) from clothes to personality to special powers to the advice and inspiration your muse would impart.

8. Memory Lane

Draw a map of your neighborhood in as much detail as you can (don't worry about scale or proportion—it's just for you). Remember the fence falling off its hinge? The old lady who stared at you from her window? The crazy dog in the yard? Now *describe* that neighborhood. Try to focus on setting and the characters in that setting, and then let the setting tease out a story. Let the truth start you on the path to fiction.

9. Your Mother Likes Him but You Don't

After you've written a description of a character, describe this character again from the point of view of a different character, like your mother, one of your friends, one of the character's friends, or a stranger.

10. A Deeper Meaning?

The theme of your story determines the story you want to tell. First, you need to think of the general topic area. Is it a story about romantic love? For example, for love, you might ask, "Why do we need to love another person?" Brainstorm themes you'd like to explore in fiction. Pick one and write a question for that topic. Now write a possible answer to that question.

11. In a Garbage Can or an Opera House?

Setting can determine the tone and mood of the story. Is your story set in the eighteenth century? Is your story contemporary, or is it set in the future? The setting of your story can reveal new details about your character to the reader. If a character was very upset and worried, would there be a pile of dishes in the sink? Write down a brief description of the world that your character inhabits, continuing to write from whatever point of view you prefer from above. Where does your character live? Where does your character work or go to school? Where is his or her favorite place to go? Orcreate a setting... He's completely lost in this world. What happens to your character when you change her surroundings?

12. Emotional Senses

Do this with a partner. Write the beginning of a scene with your main characters. Trade journals with your partner. Write down an emotion and a sense. Trade journals back. Now, continue to write your scene, trying to incorporate that emotion and that sense.

13. You Talking to Me?

A new character enters the scene and asks something unexpected. How does your character respond, and what does that reveal about the characters and their relationship or conflict? Dialogue can be a very powerful tool, so use it in small doses. No chit-chat or small talk allowed!

14. Superpowers, Anyone?

You are a superhero. What are your powers and what do you use them for? Give us all the details, from your name to your convictions. Use elements from your own life and play with them. Don't worry about starting from the beginning; just start writing what comes to you first.

Poetry Zippers:

1. Extra! Extra!

Sometimes, inspiration comes delivered to your doorstep. Take a look through the newspaper and write a poem about a person or event (or comic strip character) you find; or pick a headline and use it for the first line of a poem.

2. My Best Friend is Like a Hamburger

Compare someone who inspires you to an object, event or place in your everyday life. Give us details about how they are the same and how they are different.

3. Talk to Me

Create a character for one of the following (or choose another): Anger, Love, Death, Nature, Sadness, Fear, Spring, Beauty, Winter, etc. Describe what they look like, how old they are, their clothes, what they carry (a book, a flower…). What does their voice sound like, what do they smell like? Have them speak and tell us something about them that we need to know, that we might not expect. (Maybe Spring hates being Spring because she never gets to see the leaves change color.) Now write a poem using what you've learned.

4. No Peeking

Close your eyes for one minute and take in all the non-visual stimuli. Now write a poem about what you just experienced. The way your breath feels moving through your body. The conversation you just overheard. The way Starbucks coffee smells.

5. Sound Editors Wanted

In movies, sounds are used to make the audience feel emotion. Just the sound of leaves crunching can make you sure a monster is about to attack. The sound's words are powerful, too. Say "whisper" and you make a whispering sound. Say "pop" and those two "p"s make a popping sound. Make a list of words where the sounds enhance the meaning of the word. Then use some of the words from your list in a poem.

6. Sometimes, Freedom can Come from Restriction.

Give yourself word limits. For example, write a poem about the last time you laughed or cried really hard, using only five words per line.

7. I Used To…

Write a poem with each line filling in the blanks of "I used to be _____ but now I am _____." ("I used to write poems, but now I just do experiments"; "I used to make sense, but now I just make poems.")

8. I Didn't Say That

Write a poem consisting entirely of things you'd like to say - but never would - to a parent, lover, sibling, child, teacher, roommate, best friend, mayor, president, corporate CEO, etc.

9. Big Ears

Write a poem consisting entirely of overheard conversation.

10. Autopilot

Trying as hard as you can not to think or consider what you are writing, write as much as you can, as fast you can, without any editing or concern for syntax, grammar, narrative, or logic. Try to keep this going for as long as possible: one hour, two hours, three hours… Don't look back, don't look up.

11. I Remember…

Write a poem where each line starts with, "I remember…"

12. ZZZZZZZ

Write a poem just when you are on the verge of falling asleep. Write a line a day as you are falling asleep or waking up.

13. The Giraffe Ate My Homework

Write a poem made up entirely of excuses. Replace overused verbs (get, went, put) with more energetic and more precise active verbs.

14. I Am.

There are a few people who don't understand who you really are. Set them straight. In this poem, declare how you see yourself, right here, right now.

Songwriting Zippers:

1. Change the Lyrics

Think of a song you know well. In your mind or out loud, (depending on whether you're alone or not!), hear the melody to that song with "la la"s instead of the lyrics. Now replace the "la la"s with your own words. Start out simple - like with a kid's song (ever notice that the alphabet is sung to the same melody as "Twinkle Twinkle?") or a TV commercial - then move on to something you might hear on the radio.

2. Write a Tribute Song

Take a famous song and change the lyrics to make it a "tribute song." Pick someone you know who has a birthday or anniversary coming up and re-write the lyrics using funny and specific things about that person, or pet, or whomever.

3. A Perfect Day….

Imagine a perfect day from your childhood – or it could be the worst day of your childhood. What happened that day to make it memorable? Picture yourself back there: What is the weather like? The temperature, the breeze, the clouds – how does your skin feel? What are the smells? What are you wearing? Who else is there? How is her/his hair fixed. What is his/her scent? What are the sounds around you? How about taste? Engage all your senses in creating the image. When you look at what you have written, is there a center to your images? What overarching image sets the theme? What phrase could capture that central image? Now you have the nugget from which a song might flow.

4. What's in a Title?

Sometimes all you need to start writing is a great title! And in the case of a song, the title usually sums it all up pretty well. Look at the songs on a CD you don't know. Pick one of the titles and write your own song. After you're done, listen to the original.

5. Singable Words

Try to make your words "singable", which means easily sung, so that they roll off the tongue with little effort when you say them out loud. Long vowel sounds ("day," "goodbye," "you") and words with "l"s, "d"s, and "n"s work well for some reason. Guttural sounds and lots of "s"s, not so much! For fun, try singing the word "squelch," holding it out as long as you can! Make a list of "l," "d" and "n" words to use in a song. Look in the dictionary to choose words you wouldn't normally choose. Write a song with those words.

Essay Writing Zippers:

1. **What is your favorite book?** How has this book influenced your outlook on life? What do you identify with the most: the setting, the characters, the theme, the era? Write two or three paragraphs about what this book means to you.

2. **For a college admissions essay,** write a 250-word piece (count the words carefully!) about what you would bring to a particular campus if admitted. How are you unique? What contributions could you bring. What goals for your studies do you have? Make the reader understand why you, as an individual, would be an asset to the campus community. For a more meaningful essay, think about a school you're interested in attending. If you're not sure what the school is like, check out their website or ask your counselor.

3. **Write a brief (three paragraphs) autobiography of your future!** Be sure to include a title and what you hope your life is like in your golden years.

4. **Write a 100-word essay about the relative who has influenced you the most,** and why. If you can't think of a relative, how about a teacher, neighbor, or friend?

5. **If you could transcend time, which era would you like to travel to?** What would you want to learn from, or teach to, the people you found there? Write a 250-word essay (five to six paragraphs) about the experience.

6. **Write a 300-word essay (at least five paragraphs) about something valuable** that you gave to someone else. Think about what circumstances led to the exchange, who was involved, and what the consequences were. How do you think this experience influenced you as a person?

7. **It's not all about classic literature and music –** modern art forms are important and influential, too! Which piece from a musical, visual or literary artist still creating today do you admire most? What is it about his or her work that you connect with? Do you think it will stand the test of time? Write a 200-word essay about the piece.

8. **Where is your home?** It could be a building, a state of mind, a gathering of people, a landscape, or a feeling that comes over you when you know you're there. Write a 300-word essay about what home means to you.

9. **What is the most challenging problem in the world today?** How would you address this problem using only the power of peer-to-peer diplomacy? Where would you begin? How would you learn more about the problem, build consensus, lobby the relevant leaders, and bring about change? Write a 500-word essay about your approach.

10. **Pack a bag for a Desert Island –** no electricity, no running water, no media. What five things would be essential to you during a one-month stay? Write a 200-word essay about how you'd spend the time and what you'd bring with you.

11. **What do you like to do for fun?** Think about the five Ws (who, what, where, when, why) and paint a picture of your most fun experience. Economy of words is important, so try to do it in just 100 words.

12. **What would your best friend tell a stranger about you?** What would your arch enemy say about you? If you don't have a best friend or an enemy, create one! Tell us both sides of your story in 200 words.

13. **Write a 300-word essay about a risk that paid off for you.** What did you do, under what circumstances? Why was it a risk? How did you prepare or find the courage to get through it? What would you advise others in your situation to do? Take the reader to the defining moment when you decided to go forward.

14. **Tell us about something (real or imaginary) that you've invented.** What problems or needs does it address? Who needs it? You or the whole world? How will life be different because of the invention? Tell the reader in 200 words.

15. **Write a 300-word essay about anything you want.** Tell a story, recite a biography, capture an important experience, be experimental, use the third person, inhabit an imaginary character, speak in a special language, relive a journey. Tell the reader the story you want them to know. This is your chance to be free – make it count!

About WriteGirl

WriteGirl is a creative writing and mentoring organization that pairs professional women writers with teen girls, and was recently awarded the Medal of Service as the California Nonprofit of the Year from Governor Schwarzenegger and First Lady Maria Shriver. Through one-on-one mentoring, monthly workshops, public readings, and publications, WriteGirl's innovative writing program offers girls techniques and insights in all genres of writing, from poetry to journalism to fiction and more. WriteGirls support, encourage, and challenge each other to express themselves, their ideas, and their dreams on paper and out loud. Through involvement in the WriteGirl program, girls develop communication and life skills, self-confidence, self-esteem, and an expanded view of themselves and their futures. WriteGirl, a project of nonprofit organization Community Partners, was founded in December 2001 in Los Angeles. WriteGirl welcomes your support and involvement: Visit WriteGirl on the web at: www.writegirl.org

About WriteGirl Publications

Since 2001, WriteGirl Publications has been publishing award-winning anthologies that showcase the bold voices and imaginative insights of women and girls. Unique in both design and content, WriteGirl anthologies present a wide range of personal stories, poetry, essays, scenes, and lyrics, as well as a selection of WriteGirl writing experiments to inspire readers to find their own creative voices.

Also from WriteGirl Publications:

SILHOUETTE: Shared Secrets from WriteGirl

BEYOND WORDS: The Creative Voices of WriteGirl

LISTEN TO ME: Shared Secrets from WriteGirl

LINES OF VELOCITY: Words That Move from WriteGirl

UNTANGLED: Stories & Poetry from the Women and Girls of WriteGirl

NOTHING HELD BACK: Truth & Fiction from WriteGirl

PIECES OF ME: The Voices of WriteGirl

BOLD INK: Collected Voices of Women and Girls

THREADS

Awards for WriteGirl Publications:

2010   *Winner, Teenage, New York Book Festival: SILHOUETTE*

2010   *Winner, International Book Awards, Anthologies-Nonfiction: SILHOUETTE*

2010   *Winner, Anthologies, London Book Festival: SILHOUETTE*

2010   *Finalist, Anthologies, ForeWord Reviews Book of the Year Awards: SILHOUETTE*

2009   *Winner, Nonfiction, Los Angeles Book Festival: SILHOUETTE*

2009   *Winner, National Best Book Awards, USA Book News: SILHOUETTE*

2009   *Silver Medalist, Independent Publisher Book Awards: LISTEN TO ME*

2009   *First Place, Anthologies, National Indie Excellence Awards: LISTEN TO ME*

2009   *2nd Place, Teenage, San Francisco Book Awards: LISTEN TO ME*

2009   *Finalist, ForeWord Magazine: LISTEN TO ME*

2009   *Runner Up, Teenage, New York Book Festival: LISTEN TO ME*

2008   *1st Place, Teenage, London Book Festival: LINES OF VELOCITY*

2008   *1st Place, Grand Prize Winner, Next Generation Indie Book Awards: LINES OF VELOCITY*

2008   *Winner, National Best Book Awards, USA Book News: LINES OF VELOCITY*

2008   *Silver Medalist, Independent Publisher Book Awards: LINES OF VELOCITY*

2008   *Finalist, ForeWord Magazine: LINES OF VELOCITY*

2008   *Honorable Mention, New York Festival of Books Awards: LINES OF VELOCITY*

2008   *Honorable Mention, New England Books Festival: LINES OF VELOCITY*

2007   *Finalist, ForeWord Magazine: UNTANGLED*

2007   *Honorable Mention, London Book Festival: UNTANGLED*

2006   *Winner, National Best Book Awards, USA Book News: UNTANGLED*

2006   *Winner, Anthologies, Writers Notes Magazine Book Award: Nothing Held Back*

2006   *Honorable Mention, Independent Publisher Book Awards: Nothing Held Back*

2005   *Finalist, Independent Publisher Book Awards: PIECES OF ME*

2005   *Finalist, ForeWord Magazine: BOLD INK*

Praise for WriteGirl Publications

"WriteGirl's wonderful, inspirational anthology [*LISTEN TO ME*] belongs in every media center, public library and creative writing class."

– VOYA magazine

"WriteGirl is a dazzling chorus of smart, tough, inspired voices of independent-minded young women."

– Carol Muske-Dukes, 2008 California Poet Laureate

"I'm always impressed with the insight and courage and skill of the writing, and I love hearing the new voices in these pages [*LISTEN TO ME*]."

– Robin Swicord, Screenwriter *(Memoirs of a Geisha, The Curious Case of Benjamin Button)*

"*Untangled* is a worthwhile and highly motivational compendium of poetry, short stories, nonfiction and dramatic excerpts from both students and teachers. Including writing experiments and insight into the creative process, this volume is a perfect fit for the high school classroom. Sharp observations abound…unconventional writing exercises…motivational quotes…nonstop inspiration."

– Publishers Weekly

"The fourth annual anthology from WriteGirl [*NOTHING HELD BACK*]…suggests that reports of literacy's death have been greatly exaggerated, that language remains a transformative force. For these girls (and their mentors), writing is a lens, a filter, a way to cut through the nonsense and see the possibilities."

– David Ulin, Book Editor, *Los Angeles Times*

"Wow! I couldn't stop reading this. Talk about goosebumps! This book [*PIECES OF ME*] will shock you – and make you think – and make you FEEL – all at the same time!"

– R.L. Stine

Pens on Fire: Creative Writing Experiments for Teens from WriteGirl

Editors:	Kim Purcell and Keren Taylor
Contributors:	Allison Deegan
	Erika Hayasaki
	Jennifer Hoppe
	Sara Kaye Larson
	Michelle Lewis
	Keren Taylor
	Katharine Taylor
	Kim Purcell
	Marlys West
Book Production Team:	Phoebe Brauer
	Cindy Collins
	Mary De La Rosa
	Elisa Delson
	Karen Disner
	Fayza A. Elmostehi
	Allison Firestone
	Cynthia Greenburg
	Reparata Mazzola
	Sara Shirrell
	Shauna Smith
	Barbara Stimson
	Rachel Wimberly
Art Direction:	Keren Taylor
Book Design:	Juliana Sankaran-Felix

Printed in the United States of America

Orders, inquiries and correspondence should be addressed to:

WriteGirl Publications
Los Angeles, California
www.writegirl.org
info@writegirl.org